The Hidden History
of the War on Voting

THE
HIDDEN HISTORY *of*
=== THE ===
WAR ON
VOTING

WHO STOLE YOUR VOTE—
AND HOW TO GET IT BACK

THOM HARTMANN

Berrett–Koehler Publishers, Inc.

Berrett-Koehler Publishers, Inc.
1333 Broadway, Suite 1000
Oakland, CA 94612-1921
Tel: (510) 817-2277
Fax: (510) 817-2278
www.bkconnection.com

ORDERING INFORMATION
Quantity sales. Special discounts are available on quantity purchases by corporations, associations, and others. For details, contact the "Special Sales Department" at the Berrett-Koehler address above.
Individual sales. Berrett-Koehler publications are available through most bookstores. They can also be ordered directly from Berrett-Koehler: Tel: (800) 929-2929; Fax: (802) 864-7626; www.bkconnection.com.
Orders for college textbook / course adoption use. Please contact Berrett-Koehler: Tel: (800) 929-2929; Fax: (802) 864-7626.

Distributed to the U.S. trade and internationally by Penguin Random House Publisher Services.

Berrett-Koehler and the BK logo are registered trademarks of Berrett-Koehler Publishers, Inc.

Printed in the United States of America

Berrett-Koehler books are printed on long-lasting acid-free paper. When it is available, we choose paper that has been manufactured by environmentally responsible processes. These may include using trees grown in sustainable forests, incorporating recycled paper, minimizing chlorine in bleaching, or recycling the energy produced at the paper mill.

Library of Congress Cataloging-in-Publication Data
Names: Hartmann, Thom, 1951– author.
Title: The hidden history of the war on voting : who stole your vote, and how to get it back / Thom Hartmann.
Description: First edition. | Oakland, CA : Berrett-Koehler Publishers, Inc., [2020] | Series: The Thom Hartmann hidden history series ; 3 | Includes index.
Identifiers: LCCN 2019030589 | ISBN 9781523087785 (paperback) | ISBN 9781523087792 (pdf) | ISBN 9781523087808 (epub)
Subjects: LCSH: Suffrage—United States—History. | Voting—United States—History.
Classification: LCC JK1846 .H37 2020 | DDC 324.6/20973—dc23
LC record available at https://lccn.loc.gov/2019030589

First Edition
28 27 26 25 24 23 22 21 20   10 9 8 7 6 5 4 3 2

Book production: Linda Jupiter Productions; *Cover design:* Wes Youssi, M.80 Design; *Edit:* Elissa Rabellino; *Proofread:* Mary Kanable; *Index:* Paula C. Durbin-Westby

To my grandson, Arthur.
May he grow up in a nation that
once again values democracy.

CONTENTS

INTRODUCTION: The Heartbeat of Democracy   1

    Control the Vote, Control the Country   4

PART ONE: The Hidden History of the Vote in America   13

    Power to the South: The Three-Fifths Compromise   14

    The Racist Legacy of a Constitutional Compromise   16

    The Founders Feared a Trump-like President—Which
    Is Why They Established the Electoral College   18

    The Electoral College and Slavery   23

    The Unique Struggles of Women and Native Americans
    to Vote   26

    The Generational Fight for Women's Suffrage   28

    Silencing and Suppressing Native Voices   30

    Madison's Warning   32

PART TWO: The Economic Royalists' Modern War on Voting   35

    Why Racists Don't Want Everyone to Vote   36

    The Racist Backlash to *Brown v. Board*   39

    Conservative Excuses for Preventing Everyone
    from Voting   41

    The Billionaires' Trick to Keep Everyone from Voting   50

    Buying Politicians, Selling Lies, and Suppressing
    the Vote   56

    The Rise of Social Issues   60

    Promoting New(t)speak   63

    The Day the Music Died   67

A New War on the Vote   69

Is Voting a Right? Should It Be?   73

Numbers, Not Voters   76

Stacey Abrams Was Robbed   78

Exit Polling around the World   87

Exit Polls in the US and Red Shift Explained   90

Voting Machines, Hacking, and Red Shift   93

Privatizing the Vote with Voting Machines   96

Suppressing the Vote with Provisional Ballots   98

Diluting the Vote with Gerrymandering   100

Depressing the Vote with Money in Politics   103

The Beginnings of a Myth: Voting Fraud   106

Voting Fraud: From Myth to Dogma   107

Kris Kobach: The Voting Fraud Myth Becomes
a Mission   111

Interstate Crosscheck and the Election Integrity Scam   114

PART THREE: Solutions   119

The GOP's Grand Stand against Voting
and Democracy   120

Republicans Oppose "For the People Act of 2019"   121

Automatic Voter Registration   124

Restore the Vote for Returning Citizens   127

End Voter Caging   130

Make Election Day a National Holiday   132

Vote by Mail   133

Extend Early Voting   136

Paper Ballots or Paper Receipts   137

Stopping Politicians from Choosing Their Own Voters   139

The Electoral College and a National Popular Vote   140

Voting Systems Shape Elections: Getting beyond Two
Parties   141

Compulsory Voting   143

DC and Puerto Rico Statehood, Splitting Up Big States   145

Get Out There, Get Active   148

Finally   148

NOTES   151
ACKNOWLEDGMENTS   161
INDEX   163
ABOUT THE AUTHOR   175

The Heartbeat of Democracy

Your vote is the most important part of the American commons.

The commons embrace those realms that we all own and jointly administer through our government. They include our air and water; our roads and skyways; the frequency spectrum we use for communication, radio, and television; our public school system; our military, police, and fire departments; the agencies we use to ensure the safety and quality of our food and medications; the systems and laws that keep people playing the game of business within legal boundaries; our jails and prisons; our oceans and public lands; and our social safety net—among other things.

In this era of rapid climate change, our atmosphere and oceans, which absorb 95 percent of the extra heat in our atmosphere, are the most critical of our commons, because they have the potential, through destabilization of weather and sea level rise, to destroy civilization and even to render our planet sterile of human life.

Because government is the tool we use to define, protect, and care for most all of our commons, government could be said to be the most important of all our commons.

And because the vote is how we determine who runs our government and what policies are employed, the vote stands as the single most important part of the commons, above even government itself. As Thomas Paine said, "The right of voting for representatives is the primary right by which other rights are protected. To take away this right is to reduce a man to slavery."[1]

Today in the United States there is a concerted and well-organized campaign to prevent some people from voting while making it more and more convenient for others. At the core of this effort are think tanks, media, publications, pundits, and politicians entirely owned or heavily influenced by a relatively small group of billionaires and corporations whose wealth and business models depend on despoiling and/or exploiting the commons for profit.

This group, operating loosely under the rubric of the Republican Party, has worked for decades to deceive people into thinking that poorly paying nonunion jobs represent freedom, that lack of health care is liberty, that protection of the environmental commons is despicable "regulation," and that people working to encourage others to participate in our democracy by voting (like, for example, the League of Women Voters) are engaging in "voter fraud" and should be harassed or prosecuted out of existence.

Today's right-left battle was seeded in 1971 when Lewis Powell, the year before Richard Nixon put him on the Supreme Court, wrote his infamous memo to the US Chamber of Commerce, imploring the very wealthy and big business to get politically active.[2] He explicitly called for a vigorous effort to take over the court system of America, which he believed was being used way too often against business and the rich by environmentalists and "consumer activists" like Rachel Carlson and Ralph Nader (whom he calls out early in the memo) and the ACLU.

Realizing that the Supreme Court had engaged in a massive power grab in 1803 with the *Marbury* decision (an entire other story in its own stead that's told in *The Hidden History of the Supreme Court and the Betrayal of America*), he knew that the nine justices had become, essentially, the new kings and queens of America with the power to second-guess and thus strike down laws passed by Congress and signed by the president, as well as create law from whole cloth (as the Court did in *Dred Scott* and *Plessy*, among others). Powell wrote,

Under our constitutional system, especially with an activist-minded Supreme Court, the judiciary may be the most important instrument for social, economic and political change.

Other organizations and groups, recognizing this, have been far more astute in exploiting judicial action than American business. Perhaps the most active exploiters of the judicial system have been groups ranging in political orientation from "liberal" to the far left.

The American Civil Liberties Union is one example. It initiates or intervenes in scores of cases each year, and it files briefs amicus curiae in the Supreme Court in a number of cases during each term of that court. Labor unions, civil rights groups and now the public interest law firms are extremely active in the judicial arena. Their success, often at business' expense, has not been inconsequential.

This is a vast area of opportunity for the Chamber, if it is willing to undertake the role of spokesman for American business and if, in turn, business is willing to provide the funds.

His memo activated a group of previously disparate conservative billionaires and their foundations, from Scaife to Coors to the Kochs. And when, two years later, the Court struck down anti-abortion laws with *Roe*, this group went into hyperdrive.

As Powell wrote, "There should be no hesitation to attack the Naders, the Marcuses and others who openly seek destruction of the system. There should not be the slightest hesitation to press vigorously in all political arenas for support of the enterprise system. Nor should there be reluctance to penalize politically those who oppose it."

Employing strategies laid out by operatives such as Jude Wanniski (the "Two Santa Clauses" plan), Paul Weyrich ("I don't want everyone to vote"), and Paul Manafort (who helped supervise the electoral strategies, including massive voter suppression, used by Presidents Gerald Ford, Ronald Reagan, George H. W. Bush, Bob Dole, and Donald Trump), preventing "undesirable" people from voting has become central to Republican victories for the past two generations.

Control the Vote, Control the Country

In 2016, 6 percent of Americans who were eligible to vote nominated Donald Trump as the GOP's presidential candidate. It was 8 percent for Hillary Clinton on the Democratic side. Trump went on to be elected president by 26 percent of eligible voters.

The modern American oligarchs have largely stayed in power using three simple elements:

- explicit and overt racism,

- massive disinformation campaigns, and
- voter suppression.

No ideas. No push for better schools, hospitals, airports, roads, or bridges, or reform of our health, energy, or financial systems. No promise of more and better jobs. None of these staples of past presidential campaigns can be found in pretty much any Republican advertising today.

Instead, the public Republican message is all about race—or the subset of race, religion ("Muslim" stands in for "brown Arab" in GOP-speak) and immigration (aka brown people from south of our border)—and socialism.

Meanwhile, Republican secretaries of state across the nation are vigorously purging voters from the rolls (over 17 million, more than 10 percent of America's active voters, in just the 2016–1018 period, according to NBC News).[3]

After the five Republican appointees on the US Supreme Court gutted the Voting Rights Act in 2013, 14 GOP-controlled states moved, within a year (some within days), to restrict access to the vote, particularly for communities of color, students, and retired people.

In North Carolina, for example, 158 polling places were permanently closed in the 40 counties with the most African American voters just before the 2016 election, leading to a 16 percent decline in African American early voting in that state. An MIT study found that, nationwide, Hispanic voters wait 150 percent longer in line than white voters, and black voters can expect to wait 200 percent longer in line to vote.

In Indiana, then-Governor Mike Pence's new rigorous voter ID law caused an 11.5 percent drop in African American voting. Students are suing for their right to vote, and retired people who no longer drive but care passionately about their Social Security and Medicare are being turned away at the polls by the hundreds of thousands because their driver's licenses have expired.

The obvious failure of 40-plus years of Reaganomics and GOP policies to maintain a functional middle class in America has been a problem for the modern GOP.

In 1974, for example, the GOP had outright control of only seven states. The message "Elect us and we'll help the rich people" didn't generally resonate with American voters. It's the reason why, outside of the fluke elections of 1946 and 1952, Democrats controlled the House of Representatives outright for three generations, from 1933 to 1996, and controlled the Senate for most of that time.

Desperate to win the presidency for the GOP in 1968, Richard Nixon went so far as to commit treason by torpedoing a peace deal that President Lyndon Johnson had worked out with the North and South Vietnamese. According to Abolhassan Bani-Sadr, then president of Iran, Ronald Reagan did the same thing by cutting a deal with Iran whereby they would hold on to the US embassy hostages until after the 1980 presidential election, torpedoing President Jimmy Carter's chances of reelection.[4]

But in 2000 the GOP changed tactics. After Reagan was almost busted for his part in Iran-Contra (he testified that he had "forgotten" about details of the program more than 80 times; his growing Alzheimer's spared him an indictment), they realized that getting busted for treason wasn't worth the risk. They needed a Plan B.

And it was deliciously simple. If most voters don't like what you're selling, then just don't let them vote.

Paul Weyrich promoted this idea back in 1980 when he was campaigning for Reagan (after cofounding the Heritage Foundation), and, indeed, many Republican luminaries (such as William Rehnquist, who went from serving the GOP by standing in polling places and intimidating Hispanic and Native American voters in the 1960s to becoming chief justice of the Supreme Court) rose up through the ranks by participating in Republican-run voter intimidation schemes.

Voter suppression became the foundational go-to tactic for the GOP in 2000.

Although the GOP attacked Democratic presidential nominee Al Gore with smear and innuendo (ridiculing him for helping write the legislation that created the modern internet, for example), the main thing that got George W. Bush into the White House was voter suppression.

His brother, Florida governor Jeb Bush, and Bush's secretary of state, Katherine Harris, threw somewhere between 20,000 and 90,000 African American voters off the rolls. They were able to get the vote close enough that five Republican appointees to the Supreme Court functionally awarded Bush the presidency. (The BBC covered this in 2001 in two major investigative reports that were seen all over the world—except on any American media.)[5]

By 2016, the Republican Party had fine-tuned its voter suppression and intimidation systems to the point that they ran like well-oiled machines in nearly 30 states. Between the 2012 and 2016 presidential elections, for example, Ohio had purged more than two million voters from its rolls, the vast majority (more than two to one) in heavily African American and Hispanic counties. The five Republican appointees on the Supreme Court ruled in 2017 that they could keep it up, and other states have since adopted their new tactic of caging voters (challenging their registration status by mailing them postcards and then striking them from the voter rolls if the postcards aren't returned).

The *New York Times* reported in 2017 that in Wisconsin, about 17,000 registered voters may have been turned away at the polls in November 2016 because they didn't have the particular types of ID necessitated by Scott Walker's new voter ID law,[6] and Ari Berman reported in the *Nation* in 2016 that as many as 300,000 Wisconsinites lacked the ability to even register to vote because of the law.[7]

It's symbiotic: Billionaires and corporations spend hundreds of millions to fund Republicans, who pass laws and tax breaks that give billions to the corporations and billionaires, who then recycle a fraction of that, mere millions, back to the legislators they own. To keep the cycle going, both must prevent people who object to this system from voting.

The American Legislative Exchange Council (ALEC), funded by the Koch network and other billionaires and big corporations, has been at the forefront of these efforts, with ALEC-affiliated Republican legislators introducing the majority of voter suppressive state laws. ALEC itself facilitated the production of voter suppressive "model legislation."

Average American voters generally don't like billionaires and corporations running politics, so the billionaires and their corporations have organized major efforts to keep those people from voting. How many people? Numbers are sketchy because Republican secretaries of state are unwilling to release purge numbers and details without being sued to do so.

In 2018, investigative reporter Greg Palast sued a number of Republican secretaries of state and got his hands on purge lists that included more than 90,000 people in largely Democratic parts of Nevada, 769,436 voters purged in Colorado, 340,134 in Georgia, 550,000 in Illinois, a large but as-yet-uncounted list from Nebraska, and 469,000 purged in Indiana.[8]

Without these major voter purges, and without the disenfranchisement of young people, old people, and poor people by voter ID laws, it's a virtual certainty that America would have had President Al Gore and President Hillary Clinton, and the Democratic Party would have a six-to-three or larger majority on the US Supreme Court.

Using voter suppression, the GOP has maintained a situation that's so hostile to workers that wages have fallen for the bottom half of American workers in the years since Reagan's 1980 election.

But the old debates keep resurfacing, with the GOP echoing the positions of the founding generation's conservatives, such as John Adams. Adams wrote in a letter to James Sullivan in May 1776,

Depend upon it, Sir, it is dangerous to open So fruitfull a Source of Controversy and Altercation, as would be opened by attempting to alter the Qualifications of Voters. There will be no End of it. New Claims will arise. Women will demand a Vote, Lads from 12 to 21 will think their Rights not enough attended to, and every Man, who has not a

Farthing will demand an equal Voice with any other in all Acts of State. It tends to confound and destroy all Distinctions, and prostrate all Ranks, to one common Levell.[9]

Echoing today's more progressive politicians, Benjamin Franklin felt that the vote should be more widely available, regardless of wealth or property ownership.

Thomas Paine agreed with Franklin and went further, outright vilifying the wealthy landowners of his time who didn't want average non-landowners to vote. "[W]ealth is no proof of moral character; nor poverty of the want of it," he wrote. "On the contrary, wealth is often the presumptive evidence of dishonesty; and poverty the negative evidence of innocence." He added, "The proposal therefore to [disenfranchise] any class of men is as criminal as the proposal to take away property."[10]

But the GOP's war on voting since the early 1970s is fundamentally about seizing control of government and thus the commons, and turning both into private profit machines, regardless of the consequences for We, the People.

Part One of this book covers the history of the vote in the United States and why this country established a representative republic with an Electoral College rather than a direct democracy.

Part Two shows how moneyed interests have used this system to perpetuate inequality that benefits the superrich and corporations while ignoring the will of most Americans. The Republican Party, through gerrymandering and other voter suppression tactics, has hijacked America's political system to favor billionaires and corporations.

Finally, Part Three of this book explores a wide set of solutions that would both extend the right to vote to all Americans and create a system to ensure that elections result in outcomes that more closely align with the preferences of the American people.

PART ONE

The Hidden History
of the Vote in America

Power to the South:
The Three-Fifths Compromise

As the drama of writing the Constitution for a new nation was going on during the summer of 1787 in Independence Hall in Philadelphia (then the home of the Pennsylvania Legislature), a different kind of drama was playing out in the streets of that city.

It was, according to the newspapers of the day and the letters sent home from delegates to the Convention, a brutally hot, muggy, mosquito-infested summer in Philadelphia. This was during a time when the mechanisms of weather were largely unknown, and superstition was thickly merged with Christianity.

Thus, on May 5, when a boy of about five years died of an apparent heatstroke, an elderly woman in town was accused of being the witch who'd cast a spell upon him. The delegates were just arriving in town for the opening of the Constitutional Convention on May 14 and no doubt noticed, as reported on May 11 in the *Pennsylvania Packet* newspaper, that the good citizens of the town grabbed the woman, known only as Mrs. Korbmacher (the German word for basket maker), on one of the main streets and tried to cut open her forehead to bleed her of evil spirits.[1]

Mrs. Korbmacher was having none of it, and she ran through the streets with an angry mob following her. A few people spoke up on her behalf but were shouted down or threatened by the crowd. At the end of the day, though, they let her live and she escaped.

She wasn't so lucky, however, on July 10.

That day was a hot and muggy Tuesday, and on Friday of that week, in frustration, Edmund Randolph would submit the "Three-Fifths Compromise" to break the debate between slave states, free states, small states, and large states on the question of how many members of the House of Representatives each state should have.

It fundamentally shaped the future governance of America, and shaped the Electoral College as well for the next 240-plus years.

But on July 10, they were still slugging it out. James Madison's notes described the scene, published in *Notes of Debates in the Federal Convention of 1787*.[2]

The proposal put on the floor by Massachusetts's Rufus King, a lawyer and member of the Continental Congress, was that the states should have representatives based on their potential white male voting population, which would have created a total of 65 House members.

King argued that although he didn't want to disenfranchise the Southern slave states, they certainly didn't have enough white citizens to justify a majority of the seats in the proposed Congress.

"The four Eastern States having 800,000 souls," he said, according to Madison, "have ⅓ fewer representatives than the four Southern States, having not more than 700,000 souls, rating the blacks as 5 for 3." This, he said, would upset the "Eastern states," who would consider themselves the "subject [of] gross inequality." While he wanted to preserve the "security of the Southern" states, there was "[n]o principle [that] would justify giving them a majority."

The representative from Massachusetts, along with most of the other Eastern and Northern states, wanted to keep the union together with the Southern slave states, Madison noted, "but did not see how it could be done."

This threw the Convention into chaos.

South Carolina's Pinckney dramatically declared that if the Northern states had such a majority over the Southern states, then the slave states "will be nothing more than overseers for the Northern States." And the Southern states had no intention of ever being under the thumb of the Northern states.

The day devolved from there.

Frustrated, they gave up the debate toward the end of the day and moved on to a series of largely typographic edits of what had already been agreed on in other areas of the Constitution.

The Racist Legacy of a Constitutional Compromise

While the delegates debated inside, outside Mrs. Korbmacher was being beaten to death by an angry and frightened mob. The heat had not relented. The mob was now sure that not only had she killed the little boy but she was trying to kill them too with the heat.

In 1787, it was widely believed among the white power structure of this country that some women were witches and that people with dark skin were lazy, stupid, incapable of feeling very much pain, and generally subhuman.

We look back on Mrs. Korbmacher's sad story with a certain bemusement. Today, we no longer kill witches—the very idea of a woman being a "dangerous" witch is considered bizarre. But racial myths are still very much a part of the American political and social mindscape.

When a black man was elected president of the United States in 2008, almost a third of the white electorate believed that it was impossible for a black man to attain such an office by his own intellect and hard work.

Instead of winning through merit, talent, and political positions, people like Donald Trump and David Duke asserted, Barack Obama must have been a stalking horse, a Manchurian candidate, raised up out of Kenya by malevolent Muslim forces and installed as a child in Hawaii to one day rule over and destroy white America.

And this wasn't a worldview held exclusively by a small group of white bigots.

In 2017, white supremacists—"some very good people," as Trump said—marched in Charlottesville, Virginia, chanting, "You will not replace us. . . . Jews will not replace us." One avowed white supremacist murdered a counterprotester. Excluding the anomaly of 9/11, white supremacist terrorists killed more Americans in the previous three decades than did any other group, but police today are more likely to investigate black groups than white supremacist ones.[3,4]

The Ku Klux Klan didn't come into its own until 1865. But its progenitors, mostly in the form of the slave patrols, were terrorizing black people with enthusiasm in 1787 and continue, under other names, to do so to this day.

On the slightly cooler morning of Friday, July 13, 1787, starting from the issue of taxation, the exhausted members of the Convention considered Randolph, James Wilson, and

Roger Sherman's Three-Fifths Compromise, and it passed unanimously.[5]

They'd solved the problem, although they'd also set up the elections of John Quincy Adams, Rutherford B. Hayes, Benjamin Harrison, George W. Bush, and Donald Trump, who all lost the popular vote but became president because they won the Electoral College.

The Founders Feared a Trump-like President– Which Is Why They Established the Electoral College

The founders and framers thought they could prevent somebody like Donald Trump from ever becoming president. They were wrong, and we're still paying the price.

It's often said that the Electoral College was brought into being to perpetuate or protect the institution of slavery, and, indeed, during the first half-century of America it gave the slave states several presidents who otherwise wouldn't have been elected.

Most of the pro-slave-state bias of the Electoral College, however, was a function of the Three-Fifths Compromise (which, until the 1870s, gave slave states more members in the House of Representatives than called for by the size of their voting public) and the decision to give each state two US senators.

But, according to the framers of the Constitution themselves, the real reason for the Electoral College was to prevent a foreign power from placing their stooge in the White House.

Today we're horrified by the idea that Donald Trump may truly be putting the interests of foreign governments ahead of our own, and that money and other efforts from multiple foreign entities may have helped him get elected.

It's shocking. Many of us never took the idea seriously when the movie *The Manchurian Candidate* came out in 1962. "What an intriguing idea for a movie," we thought, "but that could never happen here."

However, this scenario was a huge deal for the founding generation. One of the first questions about any candidate for president was "Is he beholden in any way to any other government?"

At the time of the Declaration of Independence, it's estimated that nearly two-thirds of all citizens of the American colonies favored remaining a British colony (Jimmy Carter's novel *The Hornet's Nest* is a great resource). There were spies and British loyalists everywhere, and Spain had staked out its claim to the region around Florida while the French were colonizing what is now Canada.

Foreign powers had us boxed in.

In 1775, virtually all of the colonists had familial, friendship, or business acquaintances with people whose loyalty was suspect or who were openly opposed to American independence.

It was rumored that Ben Franklin, while in Paris, was working as a spy for British intelligence, and his close associate, Edward Bancroft, actually was.[6] Federalists, in particular, were wary of his "internationalist" sentiments.

Thomas Jefferson lived in France while the Constitution was drafted, and his political enemies were, even then, whispering that he had, at best, mixed loyalties (and it got much louder around the election of 1800). In response, he felt the need to protest to Elbridge Gerry, in a letter on January 26, 1799, "The first object of my heart is my own country. In that is embarked my family, my fortune, and my own existence."[7]

When John Adams famously defended British soldiers who, during an anti-British riot on March 5, 1770, shot and killed Crispus Attucks and four others, he was widely condemned for being too pro-British. The issue recurred in 1798 when he pushed the Alien and Sedition Acts through Congress over Vice President Thomas Jefferson's loud objections. British spy Gilbert Barkley wrote to his handlers in London that Quakers and many other Americans considered Adams an enemy to his country.

When Adams blew up the XYZ Affair and nearly went to war with France, his political opponents circulated the rumor that he was doing it only to solidify his "manly" and "patriotic" credentials. Historian and author John Ferling, in his book *A Leap in the Dark: The Struggle to Create the American Republic*, writes that Adams's anti-British rhetoric worked at changing the perception of him: "By mid-1798 he was acclaimed for his 'manly fortitude,' 'manly spirited' actions, and 'manly independence.'"[8]

After the Revolutionary War, the nation was abuzz about Benedict Arnold—one of the war's most decorated soldiers and once considered a shoo-in for high elected office—selling out to the British in exchange for money and a title.

So it fell to a fatherless man born in the West Indies to explain to Americans that the main purpose of the Electoral

College was to make sure that no agent of a foreign government would ever become president.

Alexander Hamilton wrote in *Federalist*, no. 68, that America was so spread out, it would be difficult for most citizens/voters to get to know a presidential candidate well enough to spot a spy or traitor. But the electors—having no other governmental duty, obligation, or responsibility—would catch one.[9]

After all, the way the Constitution set up the Electoral College, the electors were expected to cast their votes for president reflecting the preferences of their states, but they didn't have to. They'd all assemble in the nation's capital and get to know the candidates, and make their own independent determinations on the character and qualities of the men running for president. They'd easily spot a foreign agent or a person with questionable sympathies.

"The most deadly adversaries" of America, Hamilton wrote, would probably "make their approaches [to seizing control of the United States] from more than one quarter, but chiefly from the desire in foreign powers to gain an improper ascendant in our councils."

But influencing public opinion or owning a senator was nothing compared with having their man in the White House. As Hamilton wrote, "How could they better gratify this, than by raising a creature of their own to the chief magistracy [presidency] of the Union?"

But, Hamilton wrote, the framers of the Constitution "have guarded against all danger of this sort, with the most provident and judicious attention."

The system they set up to protect the presidency from an agent of a foreign government was straightforward, Hamilton claimed. The choice of president would not "depend on any preexisting bodies of men, who might be tampered with beforehand to prostitute their votes." Instead, the Electoral College would be made up of "persons [selected] for the temporary and sole purpose of making the appointment."

The electors would be apolitical, Hamilton wrote: "And they have excluded from eligibility to this trust, all those who from situation might be suspected of too great devotion to the President in office. No senator, representative, or other person holding a place of trust or profit under the United States, can be of the numbers of the electors." This, Hamilton was certain, would eliminate "any sinister bias."

Rather than average but uninformed voters, and excluding members of Congress who might be subject to bribery or foreign influences, the electors would select a man for president who was brave of heart and pure of soul.

"The process of election [by the Electoral College] affords a moral certainty," Hamilton wrote, "that the office of President will never fall to the lot of any man who is not in an eminent degree endowed with the requisite qualifications."

Indeed, although a knave or rogue or traitor might fool enough people to ascend to the office of mayor of a major city or governor of a state, the Electoral College would likely ferret out such a traitor.

"Talents for low intrigue, and the little arts of popularity, may alone suffice to elevate a man to the first honors in a single State; but it will require other talents, and a different kind of merit, to establish him in the esteem and confidence" of the men in the Electoral College, who would select him as president "of the whole Union."

Hamilton asserted, "It will not be too strong to say, that there will be a constant probability of seeing the station filled by characters pre-eminent for ability and virtue."

Unfortunately, that's not what happened.

Because of the Three-Fifths Compromise, which gave more electors to the slave states than their voting populations would indicate, the Electoral College handed the White House to four Virginia slaveholders among our first five presidents. Since that Compromise was eliminated, it has continued to wreak mischief by putting George W. Bush and Donald Trump into office.

Hamilton never envisioned a day when a man so entangled in financial affairs with foreign governments as Donald Trump is could even be seriously considered. And, by Hamilton's standards, the electors totally failed in their job in the 2016 election.

The Electoral College was a compromise designed to keep the president above political considerations; it was sold to the public as a way to prevent an agent (witting or unwitting) of a foreign power from becoming president.

It's failed on both counts.

The Electoral College and Slavery

It's as difficult to disentangle racism from birtherism as it is tough to separate the Three-Fifths Compromise from the Electoral College.

The Three-Fifths Compromise gave a larger share of representation in Congress to slave states. And because the Electoral College reflects the makeup of Congress, one could argue that were it not for slavery, George W. Bush and Donald Trump never would have become president.

Slavery has been the single largest defining factor in the history and arc of American politics. That salient "peculiar institution" is responsible for the Second Amendment and for the Electoral College working the way it does.

When Congress repealed the Three-Fifths Compromise with the 14th Amendment in the wake of the Civil War, it actually increased the federal political power of the former slave states. Instead of Southern black populations being counted at three-fifths, they were counted at 100 percent. This in turn increased the total number of members of the House of Representatives, and thus the number of Electors, from Southern states, even while those states aggressively suppressed the votes of black residents.

But the biggest perversion of democracy due to the Electoral College involves the US Senate.

For every member of Congress, there's a member of the Electoral College. At the level of the House of Representatives, this basically tracks the populations of the states. With the Senate, though, the result heavily favors the former slave states and small-population states like Wyoming and Vermont.

California, for example, has nearly 40 million citizens but only two senators. Ditto for New York, with 19 million citizens and two senators.

The imbalance is so bad that the 25 smallest states control half of the Senate (50 out of 100 senators) but represent only 16 percent of American voters. They can (and regularly do) overrule the sentiments of the other 84 percent of Americans represented by the senators from the largest 25 states.[10]

Like the Three-Fifths Compromise, the form of the Senate was the result of slavery as much as it was a conflict between large and small states. After all, several of the slave states, when their black population was excluded, had a similar number of white male voters as the medium-sized Northern states.

Samuel Thatcher of Massachusetts objected bitterly, saying, "The representation of slaves adds thirteen members to this House in the present Congress, and eighteen Electors of President and Vice President at the next election."[11]

Nonetheless, America continued to elect slaveholders to the White House all the way through the presidency of Andrew Jackson, in large part because of both the undemocratic nature of the Senate and the Three-Fifths Compromise.

The 15th Amendment resolved the three-fifths issue on paper, but the issue of how each state having two senators skewed the Electoral College persisted.

In 1934, the Senate came within two votes of the two-thirds necessary to pass a constitutional amendment to the states to eliminate the Electoral College and go to direct election of the president. Senator Alben Barkley, D-Kentucky (later Harry Truman's vice president), stated, "The American people are qualified to elect their president by a direct vote, and I hope to see the day when they will."[12]

The Senate took up the issue again in 1979, led by Senator Birch Bayh, D-Indiana, but this time it fell even shorter of two-thirds: the vote was 51 for and 49 against.

Given that as many as 80 percent of Americans currently think the Electoral College should be abolished,[13] a number of states have adopted a non-amendment alternative solution, although it's facing strong headwinds from Republican-controlled states.

From 1790 to 2016, Philip Bump wrote in the *Washington Post*, "the most populous states making up half of the country's population have *always* been represented by only about a fifth of the available Senate seats."[14]

And while the Senate has always skewed the politics of America toward the wishes of the small states, it also distorts the Electoral College, since even the smallest states have two US senators who are represented in the Electoral College vote. It's a small advantage, but it's enough to swing elections.

The Unique Struggles of Women and Native Americans to Vote

Wealthy white men have had the right to vote in America since the beginning of our republic. It's been a very, very different story for women and Native Americans.

Women's voting rights took a long time. Native Americans' took longer.

The struggle for women's voting rights began in April 1776, when 32-year-old Abigail Adams sat at her writing table in her home in Braintree, Massachusetts, a small town a few hours' ride south of Boston.

The Revolutionary War had been going on for about a year. A small group of the colonists gathered in Philadelphia to edit Thomas Jefferson's Declaration of Independence for the new nation they were certain was about to be born, and Abigail's husband, John Adams, was among the men editing that document.

Abigail had a specific concern. With pen in hand, she carefully considered her words. Assuring her husband of her love and concern for his well-being, she then shifted to the topic of the documents being drafted, asking John to be sure to "remember the Ladies, and be more generous and favourable to them than [were their] ancestors."[15]

Abigail knew that the men drafting the Declaration and other documents leading to a new republic would explicitly define and extol the rights of men (including the right to vote) but not of women. She and several other well-bred women were lobbying for the Constitution to refer instead to persons, people, humans, or "men and women."

Her words are well preserved, and her husband later became president of the United States, so her story is better known than those of most of her peers.

By late April, Abigail had received a response from John, but it wasn't what she was hoping it would be. "Depend on it," the future president wrote to his wife, "[that we] know better than to repeal our Masculine systems."[16]

Furious, Abigail wrote back to her husband, saying, "If perticular [sic] care and attention is not paid to the Ladies, we are determined to foment a Rebellion."

Abigail's efforts were unrewarded.

Adams, Jefferson, Hamilton, and the other men of the assembly wrote, "We hold these truths to be self-evident, that all men are created equal, that they are endowed by their Creator with certain unalienable Rights, that among these are Life, Liberty and the Pursuit of Happiness. That to secure these rights, Governments are instituted among Men, deriving their just Powers from the Consent of the Governed . . . "

The men had won.

At that time, a married woman couldn't make out a will because she couldn't independently own property. Her husband owned anything she'd brought into the marriage. If he died, a man appointed by a court would decide which third of her husband's estate she could have and how she could use it, and he would supervise her for the rest of her life or until she remarried. A woman couldn't even sue in court, except using the same laws applied to children and the mentally disabled with a male executor in charge.

And, for sure, a woman couldn't vote.

The Generational Fight for Women's Suffrage

Nearly a hundred years later, things hadn't changed much. Susan B. Anthony went to her ward's polling station in Rochester, New York, on November 1, 1872, and cast a vote.

Justifying her vote on the grounds of the 14th Amendment, Anthony wrote, "All persons are citizens—and no state shall deny or abridge the citizen rights."[17]

Six days later, she was arrested for illegally voting. The judge, noting that she was female, refused to allow her to testify, dismissed the jury, and found her guilty.

A year later, in the 1873 *Bradwell v. State of Illinois* decision, concerning the attempt of a woman named Myra Bradwell to practice law in Illinois, the US Supreme Court ruled that women were not entitled to the full protection of persons for purposes of voting or even to work outside the home.

Justice Joseph P. Bradley wrote the Court's concurring opinion, which minced no words: "The family institution is repugnant to the idea of a woman adopting a distinct and independent career from that of her husband. So firmly fixed was this sentiment in the founders of the common law that it became a maxim of that system of jurisprudence that a woman had no legal existence separate from her husband, who was regarded as her head and representative in the social state."[18]

After another 50 years, suffragettes eventually won the right to vote with the passage of the 19th Amendment in 1920. But burdensome laws, written and passed mostly by men, continue to oppress women to this day. These include voter suppression laws that hit women particularly hard in Republican-controlled states.

Those states, specifically, are the places where "exact match" and similar ALEC-type laws have been passed forbidding people to vote if their voter registration, ID, or birth certificate is off by even a comma, period, or single letter. The impact, particularly on married women, has been clear and measurable. As the National Organization for Women (NOW) details in a report on how Republican voter suppression efforts harm women:

Voter ID laws have a disproportionately negative effect on women. According to the Brennan Center for Justice, one third of all women have citizenship documents that do not identically match their current names primarily because of name changes at marriage. Roughly 90 percent of women who marry adopt their husband's last name. That means that roughly 90 percent of married female voters have a different name on their ID than the one on their birth certificate. An estimated 34 percent of women could be turned away from the polls unless they have precisely the right documents.[19]

MSNBC reported in a 2013 article titled "The War on Voting Is a War on Women," "[W]omen are among those most affected by voter ID laws. In one survey, [only] 66 percent of women voters had an ID that reflected their current name, according to the Brennan Center. The other 34 percent of women would have to present both a birth certificate and proof of marriage, divorce, or name change in order to vote, a task that is particularly onerous for elderly women and costly for poor women who may have to pay to access these records."[20] The article added that women make up the majority of student, elderly, and minority voters, according to the US Census Bureau. In every category, the GOP wins when women can't vote.

Silencing and Suppressing Native Voices

Republicans generally are no more happy about Native Americans voting than they are about other racial minorities or women. Although Native Americans were given US citizenship in 1924 by the Indian Citizenship Act, that law did not grant them the right to vote, and their ability to vote was zealously suppressed by most states, particularly those like North Dakota, where they made up a significant share of the nonwhite population.

Congress extended the right to vote to Native Americans in 1965 with the Voting Rights Act, so states looked for other ways to suppress their vote or its impact. Gerrymandering was at the top of the list, rendering their vote irrelevant. But in the 2018 election, North Dakota took it a step further.

Most people who live on the North Dakota reservations don't have separate street addresses, as most tribes never adopted the custom of naming streets and numbering homes. Instead, people get their mail at the local post office, meaning that everybody pretty much has the same GPO address. Thus, over the loud objections of Democratic lawmakers, the Republicans who control that state's legislature passed a law requiring every voter to have his or her own unique and specific address on his or her ID.[21]

Lots of Native Americans had a driver's license or even a passport, but very few had a unique street address. When the tribes protested to the US Supreme Court just weeks before the election, the conservatives on the Court sided with the state.[22]

In South Dakota, on the Pine Ridge Reservation, the Republican-controlled state put polling places where, on average, a Native American would have to travel twice as far as a white resident of the state to vote. And because that state's ID laws don't accept tribal ID as sufficient to vote, even casting an absentee ballot is difficult.[23]

Although the National Voter Registration Act of 1993, also known as the Motor Voter Act, explicitly says that voting is a right of all US citizens, that part of that law has never been reviewed by the Supreme Court and thus is largely ignored by most GOP-controlled states. As a result, you must prove your innocence of attempted voting fraud instead of the state proving your guilt.

Madison's Warning

Looking back, although about half of the founders were practicing their own form of voter suppression as slaveholders, they held egalitarian values for the future of this country and worried obsessively about a takeover by the very rich. It's hard to imagine that they'd ever sanction interpreting the First Amendment as a license for billionaires and corporations to buy our political system (as the Supreme Court first did in 1976 in the *Buckley v. Valeo* case and then supercharged in 2010 with *Citizens United v. FEC*).

In the summer of 1785, James Madison was essentially running the Constitutional Convention in Philadelphia, and he gave a speech (you can read it in his *Notes of Debates in the Federal Convention of 1787*) about the importance of not allowing the new country they were forming to become an oligarchy that was run of, by, and for the rich.[24] He said in a 1788 speech that there were "two cardinal objects of Government, the rights of persons, and the rights of property."[25] He added that if only the rights of property were written into the Constitution, the rich would ravage the few assets of the poor. "Give all power to property," he said, "and the indigent will be oppressed."

In fact, Madison noted, all the former republics that they had studied in his five years of preparation for writing our Constitution had ended up corrupted by the political power of concentrated money. "In all the Governments which were considered as beacons to republican patriots and lawgivers," he said, "the rights of persons were subjected to those of property. The poor were sacrificed to the rich."

Thus, wanting to establish a country where the rich didn't end up running it as their own private kingdom or oligarchy, he proposed that the House of Representatives—the only branch elected directly by the people, and every two years at that—should solely have the power to raise taxes and spend federal funds. And he didn't want the ability to vote for members of Congress to be limited to those who owned property. When that had happened, in previous governments, Madison pointed out, "the poor were sacrificed to the rich."

"The time to guard against this danger is at the first forming of the Constitution," he said in his speech. "Liberty not less than justice pleads for the policy here recommended. If *all* power be suffered to slide into hands [of property owners]," he warned, the American citizenry would "become the dupes and instruments of ambition, or their poverty and independence will render them the mercenary instruments of wealth. In either case liberty will be subverted; in the first by a despotism growing out of anarchy, in the second, by an oligarchy founded on corruption."

And, indeed, the delegates assembled agreed. Only the House of Representatives, to this day, can raise taxes and spend money.

In a 1787 letter to Edward Carrington, Jefferson wrote, "It seems to be the law of our general nature, in spite of individual exceptions; and experience declares that man is the only animal which devours his own kind, for I can apply no milder term to the governments of Europe, and to the general prey of the rich on the poor."[26]

In an 1816 letter to Samuel Kercheval, Jefferson explained, "I am not among those who fear the people. They, and not the rich, are our dependence for continued freedom."[27] He added that if we ended up with an oligarchic government that was run, directly or indirectly, by the rich, America's working people "must come to labor sixteen hours in the twenty-four . . . and the sixteenth being insufficient to afford us bread, we must live, as they [poor Europeans] now do, on oatmeal and potatoes; have no time to think, no means of calling the mismanagers to account; but be glad to obtain subsistence by hiring ourselves to rivet their chains on the necks of our fellow sufferers."

One wonders how the employees of the giant corporations that throw so much money at the Republican Party would compare that metaphor with their own current existence, since the GOP has successfully fought any meaningful reform of union rights, universal health care, or the minimum wage since the Reagan administration.

Part Two exposes the concerted strategy that transformed America into an oligarchy that serves the rich, and not we, the people.

The Economic Royalists' Modern War on Voting

Why Racists Don't Want Everyone to Vote

Before considering the details of how Republicans have, for the past 40-plus years, waged a war against the right to vote for all but wealthy white people (and why Democrats did the same before the GOP picked up the mantle), it's important to understand why each party historically has worked to manipulate the electorate to its own favor.

The Democratic Party's antipathy toward voting had roots deep in the 19th century, in the years following the Civil War. That war, and the subsequent 13th, 14th, and 15th Amendments to the Constitution pushed through by Abraham Lincoln's Republicans, gave pretty much all adult men, regardless of race, the right to vote.

Thomas Jefferson had founded the Democratic Party (it was then called the Democratic Republican Party, but the "Republican" part was dropped in the late 1820s and early 1830s), and throughout the 19th century that party (as opposed to the Whigs and the Republicans) was closely associated with support for slavery.

After the Civil War, the Democratic Party was where ex-Confederates and racist Southern whites found a home, because the anti-slavery faction that took over the Republican Party during Lincoln's presidency—the "Radical Republicans" of the 1860s and 1870s—worked hard to bring about black voting rights, particularly in the South.

Right up until the 1960s, the Democratic Party was home to the most racist of our politicians and political positions. George Wallace was elected governor of Alabama in 1962, calling, in his inaugural address, for "segregation now, segregation tomorrow, segregation forever"; he had a strong enough base in the Democratic Party in the South to challenge Lyndon Johnson in the 1964 Democratic Party primary.

Then the party went through a sea change. It started in 1964 when President Johnson signed the Civil Rights Act, and it was amplified in 1965 when he signed the Voting Rights Act.

When the Civil Rights Act was brought to the floor of the Senate for a full debate on March 30, 1964, Senator Richard Russell, D-Georgia, launched a filibuster to block it. His famous statement was simple and straightforward: "We will resist to the bitter end any measure or any movement which would have a tendency to bring about social equality and intermingling and amalgamation of the races in our states."[1]

Millions of Southern white voters deserted the Democratic Party over the issue, along with a number of politicians. Senator Strom Thurmond of South Carolina, Senator Jesse Helms of North Carolina, and Virginia governor Mills E. Godwin, for example, all became Republicans when the Democratic Party embraced voting and civil rights for African Americans and other people of color.

But it was largely a regional split in the Democratic Party: Northern Democrats supported integration, while Southern Democrats opposed it. Congress reflected the split: 95 percent of Northern Democrats in the House and 98 percent in the Senate voted for the Civil Rights Act; but among Democrats representing former Confederate states, 9 percent voted for it in the House and 5 percent voted for it in the Senate. Perhaps a harbinger of things to come, zero percent of the former-Confederate-state Republicans voted for the legislation.[2]

Bill Moyers, who was then an aide to President Johnson, wrote in his 2004 book *Moyers on America*, "When he signed the act he was euphoric, but late that very night I found him in a melancholy mood as he lay in bed reading the bulldog edition of the *Washington Post* with headlines celebrating the day. I asked him what was troubling him. 'I think we just delivered the South to the Republican party for a long time to come,' he said."[3]

Indeed, Johnson's concerns came true: Within a generation, the reliably Democratic South had become solidly Republican, almost entirely over the issue of race.

Richard Nixon exploited this with his 1968 "Southern strategy," which targeted racist Southern whites with the message that the Republican Party was their only safe harbor, now that the Democrats had abandoned segregation.

Ronald Reagan amplified the message in 1980 when he gave his first official campaign speech, focusing on states' rights, to an all-white audience near Philadelphia, Mississippi, the town portrayed in *Mississippi Burning* where three civil rights workers had been brutally murdered in 1964.

Donald Trump Jr. echoed the event with his coming-out speech in the same venue in 2016, in front of an all-white crowd sporting Confederate battle flags. "I believe in tradition," Trump Jr. said. "I don't see a lot of the nonsense that's been created about that. I understand how some people feel, but . . . There's nothing wrong with some tradition."

He added, with a metaphorical nod to the Southern strategy, "It's sort of amazing to be on this very stage where Ronald Reagan talked so many years ago."[4]

The Racist Backlash to *Brown v. Board*

The history behind the elaborate techniques that today's Republican Party uses to suppress black and Latinx votes is rooted in the "Massive Resistance" movement in reaction to *Brown v. Board of Education* that has also led to systemic resegregation.

Although the end of the Civil War and the passage of the 13th, 14th, and 15th Amendments were, in theory, supposed to grant equal status and station between black and white citizens, that is not the case to this day. After the 1896 *Plessy v. Ferguson* Supreme Court decision, which determined that "separate but equal" met the "equal protection" demands of the 14th Amendment, virtually every public school system in America that hadn't already been segregated along racial lines set out to do so.

Thus, in 1953 the case of Linda Brown, a black child who'd been assigned to the all-black Monroe Elementary School in Topeka, Kansas, came before the Supreme Court. Linda had to walk past a nearer white school to get to Monroe, and her father, Oliver Brown, knowing from his own experience the impact of racial segregation on education, joined with the NAACP to bring the case to the Court.

On May 17, 1954, a unanimous Court ruled that Linda Brown should have the right to attend the closer all-white school—and, striking down *Plessy*, ruled for the first time since Reconstruction that separate did not, in fact, mean equal.

The white supremacist political structure, particularly in the former slave states, immediately went into a frothing fury:

as the lead plaintiffs' attorney, Thurgood Marshall for the ACLU, said, "The fight has just begun."[5] Senator James Eastland, D-Mississippi, proclaimed, "The South will not abide by nor obey this legislative decision by a political body," defying the ruling while taking a swipe at the Court.[6]

Senator Harry Byrd, D-Virginia, vowed to block the *Brown* decision legislatively, and within 20 months he had organized what he called a nationwide program of Massive Resistance, including a collection of laws that would pull funding from any public school that was integrated. His 1956 "Southern Manifesto" was signed by 82 US representatives and 19 US senators. It urged former slave states to use "all lawful means" to resist integration of their schools.

In 1957, citing *Brown*, nine black students attempted to integrate Central High School in Little Rock, Arkansas. The backlash from local whites was so massive and potentially violent that President Eisenhower called out the National Guard to protect the students. That led to the Court's reaffirming its stand in *Brown* in the 1958 *Cooper v. Aaron* decision.

Across the South, local groups of whites established "private academies" to educate their children. For example, on May 1, 1959—following a court order to integrate its schools—Virginia's Prince Edward County closed its entire countywide public school system and kept it closed for a full five years.

It wasn't until President Lyndon Johnson pushed through the 1964 Civil Rights Act that there was a specific legislative remedy for school segregation. That year, most black students still attended all-black schools. But after the Civil Rights Act passed, nearly a third of black students were attending integrated schools within five years; and by 1973, the number had reached 90 percent.[7]

The past few decades have seen a steady slide back from that 1973 peak, and the foundations of *Brown* were severely shaken in a 2007 Supreme Court case combining *Meredith v. Jefferson County Board of Education* and *Parents Involved in Community Schools v. Seattle School District No. 1*.[8] In a 5–4 decision, the Court's conservative members agreed with Chief Justice John Roberts that "[t]he way to stop discrimination on the basis of race is to stop discriminating on the basis of race."

In other words, no more mandated busing or other efforts to bring black and white students together.

Justices Stevens and Breyer wrote—and delivered from the bench with unusual ferocity—scathing dissents much like those from a later Court in 2013 when Chief Justice Roberts proclaimed, while gutting the Voting Rights Act, that discrimination in America was essentially over and no longer needed legislative remedies.

In the years since Roberts and his conservative colleagues gutted *Brown*, America's schools have been segregating again. Today, black students who go to integrated schools typically attend schools where only 29 percent of their peers are white.[9]

Conservative Excuses for Preventing Everyone from Voting

In late February 2019, former Maine governor Paul LePage, a Republican, went on a local radio show to talk politics. The topic of abolishing the Electoral College came up, and LePage essentially freaked out. A national popular vote for president, LePage said, would be tantamount to turning America into a "dictatorship," and the types of people voting would prefer "the constitution of Venezuela" to that of the United States.

Why? Because, LePage said, echoing an old GOP line rarely spoken in public, if the actual vote reflected the actual public, "it's only going to be the minorities who would elect. It would be California, Texas, Florida." And those states are filled with Latinx and black people. Speaking of the movement to end the Electoral College, LePage said, "What would happen if they do what they say they're gonna do, white people will not have anything to say."[10]

There are basically three types of people—or three movements—interested in limiting the voting public to white people and, even at that, to discouraging young, old, and working-class white people from voting just as aggressively as they want to prevent people of color from voting.

They can be referred to with the shorthand labels of *Calvinists, libertarian oligarchs*, and *white supremacists*. There is, of course, considerable overlap among the three, but generally the arguments made—and legislation and policy advanced— reflect one of these three core belief systems.

THE CALVINISTS

The Calvinists have a worldview similar to that of the followers of French theologian John Calvin, who adopted the precepts of a new offshoot of Christianity around 1520 in Geneva.

Central to the idea of Calvinism are the doctrines of "total depravity" and "unconditional election." Calvinism asserted that because we are each born out of a woman's womb, we're all "dead" in sin (totally depraved) and unable to save ourselves. Instead of salvation coming from confession or good works, Calvin taught, only his god could decide (unconditionally elect) who would be saved and who would eventually rot in hell.[11]

This solved a big problem for many of the royal families of Europe in the 16th and following centuries: how to use Christianity (denial of which was a capital crime across most of Europe) to justify their absolute rule over their subjects.

If Calvin's god decided who was to be saved and who was to burn even before birth, how then could mankind separate the saved from the sinners and the noble from the wicked?

The answer was simple: the outward sign of Calvin's god's election or salvation was *wealth*. Since his god controlled everything and man was without agency, then through "irresistible grace" (the fourth of five Calvinist doctrines) Calvin's god's will would be shown to all by virtue of earthly riches and political power.

People were rich and in charge because they were blessed by God and, as Paul wrote in Ephesians 1:4–6, chosen by him "before the foundation of the world."

Modern-day conservatives like William F. Buckley and George Will advocate a secular version of Calvinism, but instead of a distant god determining who should rule, DNA would do it: the smart should be in charge, and the dumb should keep their mouths shut and, preferably, not vote or participate in politics at all.

Herbert Spencer, in his 1842 treatise *The Proper Sphere of Government*, made essentially this same argument, suggesting that while happiness and safety in society were the goals of political activity, they had to be guided by people who had the best DNA (using modern shorthand) and thus should be political leaders.[12] (He also argued in the treatise that government should never provide for education or health care—a conservative ahead of his time.)

Spencer's ideas led directly to Francis Galton's invention of the word *eugenics* in his 1869 book *Hereditary Genius: An Inquiry into Its Laws and Consequences*.[13] Eugenics held that sterilizing or even killing of what have often been described as defective or substandard people would weed out our gene pool and improve the overall intelligence and fitness of the human race in both current and future generations.

Eugenics was enthusiastically adopted by Winston Churchill, who tried unsuccessfully to make it law in Great Britain in 1912, and Woodrow Wilson,[14] who promoted it heavily in the United States during his presidency, leading every state in the union to put compulsory sterilization laws or policies into effect.[15]

Adolf Hitler, of course, picked up Churchill's and Wilson's slogans almost verbatim and applied them to Jews, Gypsies, the mentally disabled, and homosexuals (in that order of aggression), leading Germany straight to the Holocaust.[16]

George Will has argued that if voting is easy and widespread, we'll experience a sort of reverse social Darwinism, causing people of poorer quality and intelligence to vote and thus screw things up. As he wrote in an article for the *Washington Post* in 2012, "As indifferent or reluctant voters are nagged to the polls—or someday prodded there by a monetary penalty for nonvoting—the caliber of the electorate must decline."[17,18]

This perspective has a long history in American politics. Alexander Hamilton and his conservative wing among the founders and framers of the Constitution believed there must be some filter to keep out what conservative John Adams called "the rabble."

Hamilton wrote, "If it were probable that every man would give his vote freely, and without influence of any kind, then, upon the true theory and genuine principles of liberty, every member of the community, however poor, should have a vote. . . . But since that can hardly be expected, in persons of indigent fortunes, or such as are under the immediate dominion of others," they should not be able to exercise the franchise.[19]

Similarly, Adams stated, "Such is the Frailty of the human heart, that very few Men, who have no Property, have any Judgment of their own." Therefore, men without property should play no role in governance, including not being able to vote.

Adams added, "[G]enerally Speaking, Women and Children, have as good Judgment, and as independent Minds as those Men who are wholly destitute of Property."[20]

Today's version of this worldview argues that, instead of through divine predestination, poor people are poor because of defective character or intellect from birth and therefore should be discouraged from voting. And because poverty is most heavily concentrated in communities of color, they are ideally selected first for voter suppression efforts.

LIBERTARIAN OLIGARCHS

Libertarian oligarchs make up the second category of people who argue against widespread voting rights (although it's not limited to the oligarchs). Libertarianism and objectivism are inherently and openly in opposition to democracy, referring to the system as "mob rule."[21]

Scottish lawyer and historian Alexander Tytler (1747–1813) is often quoted as expressing a similar sentiment. A meme attributed to him began circulating around the time of Reagan's first election (which was about 200 years after the establishment of the United States) and exploded across the internet during the 2000 election:

> *The average age of the world's greatest civilizations from the beginning of history has been about 200 years. During those 200 years, these nations always progressed through the following sequence: From bondage to spiritual faith; From spiritual faith to great courage; From courage to liberty; From liberty to abundance; From abundance to selfishness; From selfishness to complacency; From complacency to apathy; From apathy to dependence; From dependence back into bondage.*

In fact, this was delivered as part of a 1943 speech by Henning W. Prentis Jr., former president of the National Association of Manufacturers, a group that, according to the Center for Media and Democracy, more recently has been heavily funded by the libertarian Koch brothers.[22,23]

This misattributed quote has had a remarkable impact and endurance, spawning a generation of libertarians and conservatives who love to cite the deadly "Tytler Cycle."[24]

Libertarianism fundamentally rejects the ability of the citizens of a nation to "vote themselves generous gifts from the public treasury" by simply banning the spending of such taxes on anything other than an army and police force. With objectivism, author Ayn Rand tried to wrap a similar sentiment in moral terms, saying that "moochers" and "looters" really have no *right* to lay their hands on the wealth produced by the "producers."

If one believes that people will always vote to take away from the "job creators" and give to the indigent voters, then there's a coherent and somewhat circular logic to the entire hypothesis, which makes it particularly seductive to young people born into the upper classes or with considerable privilege.

For this reason, Republicans made the "they must have skin in the game" argument every few years to object to everything from Medicare in the 1960s, to virtually every social welfare program to come out of the Great Society, to the Affordable Care Act in 2009.

For example, Walter E. Williams wrote in the conservative publication *Townhall*, "A very disturbing and mostly ignored issue is how absence of skin in the game negatively impacts the political arena. It turns out that 45 percent of American households, nearly 78 million individuals, have no federal income tax obligation." Calling this "a serious political problem," Williams concluded that "Americans with no federal income tax obligation become natural constituencies for big-spending politicians."

Williams—one among thousands of conservative writers who express similar sentiments online—wrapped up his op-ed by musing that "[s]ometimes I wonder whether one should be allowed in the game if he doesn't have any skin in it."[25]

WHITE SUPREMACISTS

White supremacists make up the final group of people who don't think everybody should have a right to vote. To justify this, they make several arguments, but all, at their core, boil down to the notion that white people are the superior race and thus should retain the majority of political power in the nation.

Most white people, particularly those older than 30, grew up exposed to racist cowboys-and-Indians shows, minstrels, and a century of movies that portrayed black people as the bad guys and white people as the winners and saviors. As a result, most white people carry a good dose of unacknowledged and often even denied-but-there-nonetheless belief in the superiority of their own race.

For example, Kali Halloway compiled research that demonstrated rather shocking, but provable, realities that have grown out of this.[26] College professors, for example, are more likely to respond to identical letters requesting mentorship from people with white male names than from people with names associated with nonwhite groups or women.[27]

White people experience less empathy when seeing black people in pain,[28] and emergency room personnel give lower doses of pain medications to people of color;[29] this belief that black people experience pain less acutely than do whites begins, among white people, around the age of seven.[30]

A UCLA study found that white people across the board, including police officers, were more likely to assume criminality when a person was black;[31] and black men, on average, get

20 percent longer prison sentences than white men for identical crimes.[32]

When, in a Stanford study, white people were told that laws like three strikes were more likely to harm black people than white people, their subsequent support for criminal justice reform dropped measurably.[33] And multiple studies have found that light-skinned African Americans are perceived as smarter and more competent than darker-skinned persons.[34]

The problem of this deep cultural (and, perhaps, human) racism that's built into all of us comes at the level of voting and governance when cynical and exploitative politicians use race as a weapon to divide people from one another, or to justify making it easier for one race to vote than another. Donald Trump's "shithole countries" epithet about black-run countries, and comments to his former attorney Michael Cohen that black people are stupid, are well-known examples of this more modern version of the openly racist public and media language of previous generations.

More subtle were Richard Nixon's "law and order" and "silent majority" campaigns, designed explicitly to mobilize white voters, a policy that has since become a staple of Republican (and some Democratic) politics.

While the idea of white superiority is apparently held by an absolute majority of whites, even if in a less-than-conscious fashion (and often by people of color as well; none of us are immune to our culture), when it's used as a political weapon, it becomes corrosive to democracy.

The Billionaires' Trick to Keep Everyone from Voting

Outside of Oprah Winfrey and Michael Jordan (and a hedge fund guy), just about all American billionaires are white. And while their white privilege helped most of them to become billionaires in the first place, for the politically active billionaires on the right, it's their money that they care about the most.

Fred Koch, the founding patriarch of the Koch family, was an early supporter of the John Birch Society (JBS), which vigorously opposed any efforts to reduce the powers of the very wealthy or elevate the wealth or political power of poor or working-class people. Their most public positions in the 1950s and 1960s were against racial integration and communism—the ultimate method for leveling the fortunes of the rich. The JBS opposed virtually all "welfare" legislation, from Social Security to Medicare to unemployment insurance, calling it socialism and equating it with a softer version of communism.

Around that same time, a Russian immigrant who'd fled the Soviet Union (her father had lost his pharmacy shop to the Bolshevik Revolution) came to America with dreams of becoming a great author or actress. Alisa Zinovyevna Rosenbaum chose the stage and pen name of Ayn Rand, and in the 1950s she wrote a rather simplistic novel celebrating inherited wealth.

In *Atlas Shrugged*, a young woman and her hapless brother inherit a railroad from their father and try to grow it over opposition from the unions, which want a safe workplace and reasonable pay. As George Monbiot wrote,

In a notorious passage, she argues that all the passengers in a train filled with poisoned fumes deserved their fate. One, for instance, was a teacher who taught children to be team players; one was a mother married to a civil servant, who cared for her children; one was a housewife "who believed that she had the right to elect politicians, of whom she knew nothing."[35]

In a subsequent novel, *The Fountainhead*, one of the "producers" of her mythology rapes a woman, but it's all good because the woman decides that she enjoys it mid-rape. Monbiot boils it down simply: "Rand's is the philosophy of the psychopath, a misanthropic fantasy of cruelty, revenge and greed."

While Fred Koch was helping the JBS in its fight against taxes and regulation, his sons were apparently reading Ayn Rand and taking her philosophy of radical selfishness to heart. They were also, by the 1970s, running the Koch oil operation and having constant struggles with regulators, particularly during the Carter administration.

Looking for political juice, David Koch joined and then largely took over the Libertarian Party in the late 1970s.

That political party had been created by the Foundation for Economic Education (FEE), a lobbying group formed in 1946 that represented the Big Three carmakers, the top three US oil companies, Monsanto, DuPont, GE, Merrill Lynch, Eli Lilly, and both US Steel and Republic Steel. Robert Welch, the founder of the John Birch Society, was on its board of directors, as were United Fruit president Herb Cornuelle; National Association of Manufacturers director and DuPont and GM board member Donaldson Brown; and Leonard Read, a long-time US Chamber of Commerce executive.

The mission of the new libertarian movement was straightforward: to lobby for the interests of big business and the uber-wealthy people that such business had created.

The same year that the FEE was created and they began the rollout of libertarianism, Congress busted an obscure University of Chicago economist named Milton Friedman for illegally shilling for the real estate industry.

As Mark Ames wrote,

> *The purpose of the FEE—and libertarianism, as it was originally created—was to supplement big business lobbying with a pseudo-intellectual, pseudo-economics rationale to back up its policy and legislative attacks on labor and government regulations.*
>
> *This background is important in the Milton Friedman story because Friedman is a founder of libertarianism, and because the corrupt lobbying deal he was busted playing a part in was arranged through the Foundation for Economic Education.*[36]

Friedman was later implicated in the aftermath of the brutal and violent takedown of democracy in Chile, and his acolytes helped privatize the state-owned properties of the Soviet Union, creating the kleptocratic and oligarchic government that now runs Russia and many of the former Soviet states. Libertarianism, it turns out, has had real-world impacts, which include the deaths of thousands.

No country has ever successfully established a libertarian form of economy or governance; it was, after all, a scam set up to front for the very rich and the corporations that made them that way. But that hasn't stopped libertarian and corporatist ideologues from trying.

While Chile and Russia are well-known examples, few Americans seem to remember how George W. Bush, Dick Cheney, and Donald Rumsfeld simply stood on the sidelines watching as the treasures of Iraq were looted after the United States took down their government.

It was to be a Grand Experiment: they'd finally prove that without government interference in a nation's economy or social systems, a utopia would emerge. L. Paul Bremer was their front man, arriving in Iraq on May 2, 2003, to begin the process of "freeing" the country's economy so that the world's corporations would flood in and create a paradise.

As Naomi Klein wrote for *Harper's Magazine* in an article titled "Baghdad Year Zero,"

> *The tone of Bremer's tenure was set with his first major act on the job: he fired 500,000 state workers, most of them soldiers, but also doctors, nurses, teachers, publishers, and printers. Next, he flung open the country's borders to absolutely unrestricted imports: no tariffs, no duties, no inspections, no taxes. Iraq, Bremer declared two weeks after he arrived, was "open for business."*
>
> *One month later, Bremer unveiled the centerpiece of his reforms. Before the invasion, Iraq's non-oil-related economy had been dominated by 200 state-owned companies, which produced everything from cement to paper to washing machines. In June, Bremer flew to an economic summit in Jordan and announced that these firms would be privatized*

immediately. "Getting inefficient state enterprises into private hands," he said, "is essential for Iraq's economic recovery." It would be the largest state liquidation sale since the collapse of the Soviet Union.[37]

Once again, Milton Friedman, the FEE's heirs, and libertarianism made a few more billionaires and destroyed the lives of literally millions of people.

The source of the funds being channeled to Friedman back in 1949 was a man named Herbert Nelson, who was the chief lobbyist and executive vice president of the National Association of Real Estate Boards, which not only was opposed to rent control laws but also had one of the largest lobbying budgets in Washington, DC.

Congressional investigators found a letter he wrote in 1949 saying, "I do not believe in democracy. I think it stinks. I don't think anybody except direct taxpayers should be allowed to vote. I don't believe women should be allowed to vote at all. Ever since they started, our public affairs have been in a worse mess than ever."[38]

Although the details are still a bit fuzzy, it appears that libertarianism (and the creation of a political party using that name) was Nelson's idea, or at least one he promoted vigorously. With a budget of over $60 million (in today's dollars), Nelson hired the FEE to come up with a third party that would argue for the interests of the wealthy developers and landlords he represented. The FEE, in turn, hired Milton Friedman.

Reason magazine, heavily funded by the Kochs, was the main voice of the libertarian movement in the 1970s, and in 1977 it published a fascinating article by Moshe Kroy that described how libertarians should market their free-market fundamentalism to skeptical Americans. Noting that it was important not to lie to people outright, Kroy wrote, "The point is that you can use tricks—and you'd better, if you really want libertarianism to have a fighting chance."[39]

The tricks involved repackaging and reframing libertarian dogma and using "salesmanship."

For example, Kroy asserted that the average person wouldn't understand an abstraction like individual rights. So don't even bother explaining how libertarianism would shrink government and empower corporations and the rich. "Instead," Kroy wrote,

> what you can do is to explain to him that libertarianism is just against one thing: CRIME. By crime you mean just what he means: theft, robbery, kidnapping, enslavement. He will of course agree, because he thinks this is obvious. Then you just explain (at great length, and with many examples) that taxation is armed robbery, that inflation through deficit spending and money printing is theft—as well as forgery of money—that draft is basically kidnapping, etc.[40]

This was something the average person could understand. The government that people thought would protect them from polluting corporations, would provide an efficient court and fiscal system to protect their jobs and bank accounts from corporate grifters, and would defend their lives in war if necessary—that government was, in fact, an evil thing.

If the billionaires could get the average American to look at government the way that oil, chemical, real estate, and banking industry billionaires did, and just elect politicians who were bought and paid for by those industries, then things would get very, very easy.

Buying Politicians, Selling Lies, and Suppressing the Vote

Right-wing billionaires know that if average Americans understood their real agenda, we'd never again elect a Republican. And it's been that way for a long, long time.

As historian, author, and University of Wisconsin professor Harvey J. Kaye wrote in 2015 for Bill Moyers's online magazine,

> *Polls conducted in 1943 showed that 94 percent of Americans endorsed old-age pensions; 84 percent, job insurance; 83 percent, universal national health insurance; and 79 percent, aid for students—leading FDR in his 1944 State of the Union message to propose a Second Bill of Rights that would guarantee those very things to all Americans. All of which would be blocked by a conservative coalition of pro-corporate Republicans and white supremacist southern Democrats.*[41]

It wasn't always this way.

In 1956, when Republican president Dwight D. Eisenhower was seeking reelection, he campaigned on a platform that bragged that the Eisenhower administration "has enforced more vigorously and effectively than ever before, the laws which protect the working standards of our people," that "unions have grown in strength and responsibility, and have increased their membership by 2 millions," and that the administration had led the "expansion of social security" and called for "better health protection for all our people."

The platform pledged that the Eisenhower administration would "continue to fight for dynamic and progressive programs," including "improved job safety of our workers." It would "[s]trengthen and improve the Federal-State Employment Service and improve the effectiveness of the unemployment insurance system"; prevent corporations from robbing pension plans by working to "[p]rotect by law, the assets of employee welfare and benefit plans"; "assure equal pay for equal work regardless of Sex"; "[e]xtend the protection of the Federal minimum wage laws to as many more workers as is possible"; and—remember that this was before Nixon's Southern strategy—"[c]ontinue to fight for the elimination of discrimination in employment because of race, creed, color, national origin, ancestry or sex."

It even went so far as to embrace increased immigration into the United States, noting that the administration had "sponsored the Refugee Relief Act to provide asylum for thousands of refugees, expellees and displaced persons" and would "continue and further perfect its programs of assistance to the millions of workers with special employment problems, such as older workers, handicapped workers, members of minority groups, and migratory workers."[42]

Eisenhower was the last Republican who was elected without having to resort to treason or election fraud, and the last Republican to talk in such a "liberal" way. Fred Koch's John Birch Society was fond of informally referring to Ike as a communist.

From the polls in the 1940s to polls today, most Americans are closer to the policy positions of Senator Bernie Sanders, I-Vermont, than to those of even moderate Democrats like former president Bill Clinton. And when presented with clear lists of Republican positions, most Americans are repelled.

So, to get people to vote for the largely Republican politicians they own, the billionaires and their front companies realized that first they must *lie*.

But even that wasn't enough.

When Reagan, in his first inaugural, said, "In this present crisis, government is not the solution to our problem; government is the problem," most Americans didn't understand that the president was setting up calls for privatizing Social Security; ending Medicare (which Reagan had campaigned against in the 1960s when it was passed); and dialing back on the pollution controls that the EPA had put into place during the Nixon, Ford, and Carter administrations. Just minutes after the Iranians released their hostages, Reagan said, "It is no coincidence that our present troubles parallel and are proportionate to the intervention and intrusion in our lives that result from unnecessary and excessive growth of government."[43]

Most Americans didn't think he meant that we should stop funding hospitals and public schools, or devastate LBJ's Great Society programs that had cut the poverty rate in America in half. They didn't see Betsy DeVos or Scott Pruitt on the horizon.

But there they were.

Ironically, in 1980, the year Reagan was first elected president, David Koch essentially outed the Libertarian Party. He made a massive donation to the party, and they put him on the ticket as vice president. And he figured that Americans were smart enough that he wouldn't have to use the salesmanship that Moshe Kroy had advocated just a few years earlier.

The Libertarian Party platform on which Koch ran in 1980 was unambiguous. It included the following:

- We favor the abolition of Medicare and Medicaid programs.
- We oppose any compulsory insurance or tax-supported plan to provide health services. . . .
- We favor the repeal of the . . . Social Security system. . . .
- We oppose all personal and corporate income taxation, including capital gains taxes.
- We support the eventual repeal of all taxation.
- As an interim measure, all criminal and civil sanctions against tax evasion should be terminated immediately.
- We support repeal of all . . . minimum wage laws. . . .
- Government ownership, operation, regulation, and subsidy of schools and colleges should be ended. . . .
- We support the abolition of the Environmental Protection Agency. . . .
- We call for the privatization of the public roads and national highway system. . . .
- We advocate the abolition of the Food and Drug Administration. . . .

- We oppose all government welfare, relief projects, and "aid to the poor" programs.[44]

The list went on from there, including ending government oversight of abusive banking practices by ending all usury laws; privatizing our airports, the FAA, Amtrak, and all of our rivers; and shutting down the Post Office. In a bone they threw to the white supremacist, white evangelical, and Catholic Christian movements, they also called for an end of all tax-supported abortions (although the Hyde Amendment had already banned this in 1976).

Koch thought they'd kicked off a movement, but when the election returns came in, he was disappointed. Commenting that he'd always been talking to friendly crowds, he candidly noted that he was surprised when his candidacy pulled only about a million votes nationwide.

So the billionaires walked away from libertarianism and turned their attention to taking over the Republican Party. That, it turned out, was much easier.

The Rise of Social Issues

In the spirit of the 1971 Powell memo, the Supreme Court, in its 1976 *Buckley v. Valeo* decision, made it legal for wealthy people to own politicians and spend unlimited amounts of money to influence elections and policy. Two years later, it extended the logic that such spending was protected by First Amendment "human rights of free speech" to corporations in *First National Bank of Boston v. Bellotti*.

Buying politicians was not only legal but astonishingly cheap: for a few hundred thousand dollars, a captive politician could shepherd through Congress legislation that would ensure *billions* of dollars in profits for his overlord corporate and billionaire donors.

The problem that the billionaires and their corporations had was that Americans were getting wise to the game. People in the United States still wanted—just as they did in the 1950s—the sort of social safety net enjoyed by the citizens of every other developed country in the world.

How could countries from Germany to Canada to Costa Rica provide a free or nearly free college education, free or very-low-cost universal health care, and excellent free public schools when we in America had over a trillion dollars in crippling student loan debt, more than 600,000 medical bankruptcies every year (the total for the other 33 of the 34 OECD "developed countries": zero), and crumbling 1960s and 1970s infrastructure from schools to roads to airports and railways?

And when David Koch came along and transparently laid out the libertarian agenda, the shock was even deeper. By the end of the Reagan administration, most Americans realized that they had little say in the fate and future of their own nation and its domestic and international policies.

A diversion became necessary. Enter "social issues."

The Supreme Court had upended the "social" hopes of white racists with *Brown v. Board* and subsequent decisions, and President John F. Kennedy's decision to force integration of schools in the South lit that torch.

The Court's *Roe v. Wade* decision in 1973 helped create a multimillion-dollar-a-year anti-abortion industry, particularly among the more cynical religious hucksters and TV preachers who began to thrive and prosper on viewer donations in a big way in the 1970s.

President Bill Clinton's 1994 passage of the assault weapons ban kicked the weapons industry and their front group, the National Rifle Association, into the big leagues of fundraising and fearmongering.

Meanwhile, as Reaganism's economic impacts spread across the country, destroying much of the white (and some of the emerging black) middle class (mostly through gutting unions and legalizing the corporate theft of pension funds), economic insecurity became widespread.

By 2000, a generation was reaching college age and discovering that they'd almost certainly never do better than their parents—a first since the Republican Great Depression of 1929 (yes, that's what they called it until after World War II).

Republicans, who had historically pointed to "liberals" calling for more unionization (the US peak, just before Reagan, was around a third of the country; most European countries are over 80 percent), an expansion of Medicare/Medicaid, and better schools, changed their sales pitch.

Liberals, they said, were fundamentally un-American. The American Dream, which the Greatest Generation had defined as a good union job with annual vacations, home ownership, and the ability to put their kids through college, was reinvented to be the lives of Bill Gates and Steve Jobs.

Every American, the Republicans told us in op-eds and on TV, wanted to become a billionaire, and every American still had that opportunity—just look at Bill Gates and Steve Jobs! If we didn't take good care of those billionaires, there may not be a money bin in the future of the average (but lucky or brilliant or inventive or lottery-winning) American.

Massive tax cuts for the very wealthy passed by Reagan, Bush Jr., and Trump—which, in total, sucked well over $20 trillion out of the economy and handed it over to the very, very, very rich—were going to stimulate the economy and expand opportunity. *Everybody* could one day become a job creator.

Promoting New(t)speak

In a pivotal 1996 memo from GOPAC, a Republican non-profit, to Republican politicians and activists distributed by Speaker of the House Newt Gingrich, R-Georgia, the speaker and his colleagues made it clear that the future of the GOP wasn't going to be in meeting the needs of average Americans; instead, they suggested, it was in *talking* in a way that would cause people to *think* the GOP was.[45]

Never again would they blunder into clear and blunt language about their true goals, as David Koch had so disastrously done in 1980.

Titled "Language: A Key Mechanism of Control," the memo declared, "We believe that you could have a significant impact on your campaign and the way you communicate if we help a little. That is why we have created this list of words and phrases."[46]

The list, the memo said, was "prepared so that you might have a directory of words to use in writing literature and mail, in preparing speeches, and in producing electronic media. The words and phrases are powerful. Read them. Memorize as many as possible."

There were two parts: "Optimistic Positive Governing words and phrases . . ." and "Contrasting words to help you clearly define the policies and record of your opponent and the Democratic party."

When discussing tax cuts or deregulation of polluting industries or cutting backdoor deals for big banks, Republican politicians should use words like *candid, common sense, crusade, dream, duty, family, freedom, liberty, opportunity, pristine, prosperity, reform, strength, tough, truth,* and *vision* (this is only a partial list).

When describing Democratic plans to extend unemployment insurance or expand unionization or build out America's infrastructure, and especially for issues like abortion, guns, gays, or God, there was a very different word list. It included "powerful words that can create a clear and easily understood contrast. Apply these to the opponent, their record, proposals and their party": *abuse, betray, bizarre, bosses, bureaucracy, corrupt, decay, disgrace, greed, hypocrisy, incompetent, liberal, pathetic, permissive, radical, red tape, self-serving, shame, sick, taxes, traitors, waste,* and the two worst: *unionized* and *welfare* (again, among other words).

Rush Limbaugh and a pack of well-funded competitors were rising fast with a little help from their friends, amplifying Newt's GOPAC word list.

Ken Vogel and Mackenzie Weinger reported in Politico in 2014 that "conservative groups spent nearly $22 million to broker and pay for involved advertising relationships known as sponsorships with a handful of influential talkers including [Glenn] Beck, Sean Hannity, Laura Ingraham, Mark Levin and Rush Limbaugh between the first talk radio deals in 2008 and the end of 2012. Since then, the sponsorship deals have grown more lucrative."[47] Most of the money was laundered (my word, not theirs) through groups like the Heritage Foundation.

"Heritage began sponsoring Hannity in 2008 and paid $1.3 million in 2011 to a broker to arrange and fund the deal, according to the group's IRS filings," Vogel and Weinger wrote. "The Koch brothers–backed Americans for Prosperity paid at least $757,000" primarily to sponsor Mark Levin's radio show, and Rush Limbaugh was "paid more than $2 million in some years and more than $9.5 million overall."

The billionaires know how to take good care of the people broadcasting their worldview virtually 24/7 in every city in America of any consequence. Nothing even close—nothing at all, frankly—existed or exists on the left side of the radio dial.

Meanwhile, billionaire Rupert Murdoch brought to the United States the same libertarian worldview he'd first inflicted on Australia and then Great Britain. Kevin Rudd, a former prime minister of Australia, wrote about Murdoch's awesome influence over that country in a blunt article for the *Sydney Morning Herald* in August 2018 titled "Cancer Eating the Heart of Australian Democracy."[48] Murdoch himself, Rudd wrote, was "the greatest cancer on the Australian democracy. Murdoch is not just a news organisation. Murdoch operates as a political party, acting in pursuit of clearly defined commercial interests, in addition to his far-right ideological world view." He pointed out that "Murdoch owns two-thirds of the country's print media."

"In Britain," Rudd wrote, "Murdoch made Brexit possible because of the position taken by his papers. In the United States, Murdoch's Fox News is the political echo chamber of the far right, which enabled the Tea Party and then the Trump party to stage a hostile takeover of the Republican Party."

Murdoch's positions weren't at all ambiguous, Rudd suggested. They were simply pro–white rich people. "In Australia, as in America," he wrote, "Murdoch has campaigned for decades in support of tax cuts for the wealthy, killing action on climate change and destroying anything approximating multiculturalism."

In fact, while liberals were scrambling to raise and then exhaust around $17 million over half a decade to put Air America on 54 radio stations nationwide (conservative talk is on more than 1,000), Murdoch apparently didn't think twice about losing nearly $100 million a year in the first few years of Fox News, according to Brit Hume. In a 1999 interview with PBS, Hume said that the channel, launched in 1996, was still in a position where it "loses money. It doesn't lose nearly as much as it did at first, and it's—well, it's hit all its projections in terms of, you know, turning a profit, but it's—it will lose money now, and we expect for a couple more years. I think it's losing about $80 million to $90 million a year."[49]

But if Murdoch could help get Republican politicians elected so that he could have billions of dollars in tax cuts and deregulation that would let him expand his empire in ways previously illegal in the United States, then spending a few hundred million to launch a nationwide propaganda operation was chump change. Eventually, it even turned into a cash cow, as had so many of his other media purchases in the US, UK, and Australia.

And if Gingrich's word list sounds familiar, it's because it lives on, in daily rants across America from Fox News to hundreds of right-wing talk hosts on radio stations owned by multibillion-dollar corporations.

The Day the Music Died

For years it worked like a charm, at least from the 1980s until around 2016. Even when Democrats did win elections, they had to eschew labels like "liberal" and take positions like Bill Clinton's infamous "the era of big government is over," as was "welfare as we know it." President Barack Obama's signature piece of legislation, the Affordable Care Act, added billions to the coffers of big insurance and drug companies and continued to legally prevent Americans who were under 65 (and not disabled) from accessing Medicare.

And then, in 2015, a real estate mogul and reality TV star burst onto the scene, blowing up the carefully crafted Potemkin village that his fellow billionaires had built over two generations.

The Republican Party was corrupt, Trump said, lying to get Americans into phony wars for political gain, cutting taxes on rich people like himself at the expense of the average guy, and fawning over phony war heroes like John McCain and low-energy hustlers like Jeb Bush and Rick Perry. The Democratic Party was rigged, too, Trump pointed out, sympathizing with Bernie Sanders, who had been almost entirely ignored by corporate media for nearly a year even as he was drawing crowds of 5,000 to 30,000 at nearly every stop.

Trump talked about giving people the universal health care they'd been yearning for since the 1940s (when the GOP first shot down Harry Truman's single-payer plan) and said he'd do so at a "lower cost" and with "better benefits" than either Obamacare or Medicare. Union jobs were going to flood back into the country. Billionaires were going to be crippled by higher Trump taxes—"I'll take a huge hit," he solemnly proclaimed.

Most of the conservative billionaire class was horrified, and the Koch network (which holds a semiannual get-together for billionaires to raise hundreds of millions to spend on politics) declined to support Trump in 2016. But a few, among them Sheldon Adelson and Robert Mercer, threw in with Trump, and with a little help from oligarchs in Russia, Saudi Arabia, and Israel, Trump ended up in the White House.

Within a year of Trump's taking over the Oval Office, and the GOP taking over both the House and the Senate, Americans began to realize that the entire thing was just another Reaganesque scam. Trump was able to hold together his base mostly by using race-based fear tactics about invading brown hordes from south of the border. He kept Republicans generally on his side by threatening to support Republican primary challengers if they didn't swear fealty.

But it wasn't enough, and the professionals in the Republican Party knew it. They could see the wipeout of 2018 coming, and it scared them to their core. Demonizing unions and universal health care didn't work anymore, because candidate Trump had called them both out as benefits. The 2017 tax cut was widely seen as a $1.5 trillion gift to the billionaire class, put on the credit card of the nation's children and grandchildren.

Even their fear tactics about black crime and invading Mexicans were backfiring, and the Supreme Court had had the gall to end the debate over gay marriage by simply legalizing it nationwide.

There was only one serious path left: figure out a way to prevent the wrong people from voting or, if they voted, to make sure their votes weren't counted.

Voter suppression and election fraud became the principal method of ensuring electoral success, buttressed by hundreds of millions of dollars in TV advertising and sophisticated online influence operations.

It was a new day for the Republican Party—one that meant going all in, nationally, at every level, to block young people, elderly people, poor and working poor people, and people of color from having a say in who represented them in government.

A New War on the Vote

While preventing people from voting has a long and sordid history in the United States (and, frankly, around the world), the modern-day Republican Party's reliance on voter suppression as a primary tool to win elections kicked off in a big way in 1993. That was the year when 27 Democrats and one Republican cosponsored HR2, the National Voter Registration Act (NVRA), sometimes called the Motor Voter Act.[50]

In the House, it got 238 Democratic votes and 20 from Republicans;[51] in the Senate, every Republican but two voted against it, while every present Democrat voted for it (Jay Rockefeller missed the vote).[52]

Several parts of the legislation freaked out the GOP, the most prominent being that it required every state to let people register to vote when they presented themselves at DMVs to apply for a new or renewed driver's license (this part is called Article 5 of the Act).

Other objectionable language in the Act included its preamble, which numerous Republicans thought might cause no end of problems if the Supreme Court were ever to try to enforce it. The preamble to the bill, now Title 42, Section 1973gg, is a long, three-part run-on sentence that says, in clear and straightforward language,

> The Congress finds that—
>
> (1) the right of citizens of the United States to vote is a fundamental right;
>
> (2) it is the duty of the Federal, State, and local governments to promote the exercise of that right; and
>
> (3) discriminatory and unfair registration laws and procedures can have a direct and damaging effect on voter participation in elections for Federal office and disproportionately harm voter participation by various groups, including racial minorities.[53]

Republicans probably could have relaxed. The only significant ruling by the US Supreme Court citing the NVRA was in 2018, in *Husted v. Randolph*, in which Justice Samuel Alito wrote the majority opinion allowing John Husted, Ohio's secretary of state, to continue with an aggressive purge of voters from that state's rolls heading toward the 2018 election.[54]

In his dissent, Justice Stephen Breyer pointed out that around 4 percent of Americans move out of their county every year. Yet "[t]he record shows that in 2012 Ohio identified about 1.5 million registered voters—nearly 20% of its 8 million registered voters—as likely ineligible to remain on the federal voter roll because they changed their residences."

Justice Sonia Sotomayor's dissent was even more scathing. "Congress enacted the NVRA against the backdrop of substantial efforts by States to disenfranchise low-income and minority voters," she wrote, "including programs that purged eligible voters from registration lists because they failed to vote in prior elections. The Court errs in ignoring this history and distorting the statutory text to arrive at a conclusion that not only is contrary to the plain language of the NVRA but also contradicts the essential purposes of the statute, ultimately sanctioning the very purging that Congress expressly sought to protect against." She quoted the NVRA's preamble and, essentially, accused the conservative majority (it was a 5–4 decision) of helping states engage in racial discrimination in the voting process.

Today's Supreme Court notwithstanding, in 1993, Republicans couldn't be so sure that the Court would uphold "the right of citizens of the United States to vote" and the "duty" of states to "promote the exercise of that right." So they came up with a story that they started selling through op-eds, in speeches, and on Fox News and right-wing talk radio.

This story was simple. There's massive voter fraud going on, where people are voting more than once in different polling places and doing so under different names. In addition, the Republican story goes, there are millions of "illegal aliens" living in the United States, and they're voting by the millions (Donald Trump asserted that it was between three million and five million in the 2016 election),[55] and they are able to vote because they're not required to show positive ID proof that they're eligible-to-vote citizens.

This was a huge step up from the old Republican strategy of simply discouraging or intimidating voters of color.

William Rehnquist, for example, was a 40-year-old Arizona lawyer and Republican activist in 1964, when his idol, Barry Goldwater, was running against Lyndon Johnson for president. Rehnquist helped organize a program titled Operation Eagle Eye in his state to aggressively challenge the vote of every Hispanic and black voter and to dramatically slow down the voting lines in communities of color to discourage people who had to get back to work from waiting hours to vote.

As Democratic poll watcher Lito Pena observed at the time, Rehnquist showed up at a southern Phoenix polling place to do his part in Operation Eagle Eye.[56]

"He knew the law and applied it with the precision of a swordsman," Pena told a reporter. "He sat at the table at the Bethune School, a polling place brimming with black citizens, and quizzed voters ad nauseam about where they were from, how long they'd lived there—every question in the book. A passage of the Constitution was read and people who spoke broken English were ordered to interpret it to prove they had the language skills to vote."[57]

Rehnquist was richly rewarded for his activism; he quickly rose through the GOP ranks to being appointed by President Nixon, in 1972, to the Supreme Court and then elevated in 1986 by President Reagan to chief justice, a position he used to help stop the vote recount in 2000 and hand the election that year to George W. Bush in the case of *Bush v. Gore*.

(Interestingly, two lawyers who worked with the Bush legal team to argue the case before Rehnquist included then-little-known lawyers John Roberts[58] and Brett Kavanaugh.[59] Bush rewarded Roberts by appointing him not just to the Court but directly to the chief justice position when Rehnquist died. Roberts was also a tie-breaking vote to allow Ohio to continue its voter purges in 2017, and he wrote the 5–4 decision that gutted the Voting Rights Act in *Shelby County v. Holder* in 2013.)

Operation Eagle Eye was one of thousands of such formal and informal operations across the United States. Even though the Republican Party was restrained by a consent decree in 1981 from such practices (and from caging), it largely ignored the consent decree and continued these sorts of practices right up until the decree was essentially overturned in the *Shelby County v. Holder* case and their efforts were legalized.[60]

Now what was once called caging—challenging voters' registration status by, for example, sending out postcards to voters and then purging them from the rolls if they fail to return the cards—has been granted the seal of approval by the Supreme Court and, in the years since *Shelby County*, has spread to nearly 20 Republican-controlled states.

All of which again raises the fundamental question: Do Americans legally have a right to vote?

Is Voting a Right? Should It Be?

The framers of the Constitution were pretty skittery about the issue. The roughly half of the Constitutional Convention that represented slaveholding states didn't want anything that might one day force their states to allow slaves to vote, and many of the Northern representatives were wary of too much democracy breaking out and leading to what John Adams referred to as "the rabble" voting. And there was an absolute consensus that women should never be allowed to vote.

Thus, voting is only really addressed in the amendments to the Constitution, and in each case very, very carefully.

The 13th Amendment says, "The right of citizens of the United States to vote shall not be denied or abridged by the United States or by any State on account of race, color, or previous condition of servitude."

Similarly, the 19th Amendment says, simply, "The right of citizens of the United States to vote shall not be denied or abridged by the United States or by any State on account of sex."

And the 26th Amendment lowers the voting age to 18: "The right of citizens of the United States, who are eighteen years of age or older, to vote shall not be denied or abridged by the United States or by any State on account of age."

But while each of these prohibits the prevention of people from voting because of their race, color, sex, or age, nowhere is there to be found in the Constitution an affirmative "right to vote" for all citizens.

To the contrary, in *Bush v. Gore*, the Supreme Court ruled that "[t]he individual citizen has no federal constitutional right to vote" for the president, because it's actually a vote by proxy in which a citizen is voting for a member of the Electoral College, who will then cast the vote that counts for president.

That, among other arguments that were hotly contested in multiple dissents by the four Democratic-appointed justices, led the logic that shut down the vote count in Florida, which would later find, when the votes were recounted by a group of news organizations a year later, that Al Gore had actually won the state and thus the 2000 election.[61]

In a similar case just a few weeks before *Bush v. Gore*, the Republican majority on the Supreme Court ruled that the Equal Protection Clause of the 14th Amendment didn't mean that we all have an equal right to vote. "The Equal Protection Clause does not protect the right of all citizens to vote," the justices affirmed in upholding a lower court's ruling that people in Washington, DC, are not entitled to representation in Congress.

As congressman and constitutional scholar Jamie Raskin, D-Maryland, wrote, while at least 135 countries have written an affirmative right to vote into their constitutions, "[by] my count, only Azerbaijan, Chechnya, Indonesia, Iran, Iraq, Jordan, Libya, Pakistan, Singapore, and, of course, the United Kingdom (whose phony doctrine of 'virtual representation' the colonists rebelled against centuries ago) still leave voting rights out of their constitutions and therefore to the whims of state officials."[62]

This led Representative Mark Pocan, D-Wisconsin (and cosponsors), to propose a simple amendment to the Constitution. In 2013, they introduced into Congress amending legislation that said, "Every citizen of the United States, who is of legal voting age, shall have the fundamental right to vote in any public election held in the jurisdiction in which the citizen resides."[63]

Speaker of the House Paul Ryan, R-Wisconsin, refused to allow it to come to the floor for a vote, and it died in that congressional session; a similar fate has befallen efforts by Democratic senators over the years.

Such an amendment would completely flip upside down virtually all of the Republican Party's many efforts to prevent people from voting. Instead of voters having to prove that they were eligible to vote, the government (from federal to state to local) would have to affirmatively prove, through due process, that they'd lost that right or weren't eligible for it (presumably by conviction for treason or loss of citizenship).

With an affirmative *right* to vote in place, Rehnquist's Operation Eagle Eye would have been illegal, as would the many state efforts to make it harder to register or to vote. It would criminalize efforts by state and local officials to close polling places, require strict IDs while closing DMVs, or arbitrarily engineer elections in ways that would make it more difficult to vote.

It would also require election officials to make sure that their operations were state-of-the-art and not vulnerable to hacking or malfeasance (particularly if the citizens' right to have their vote counted was included in the amendment). Ending the Electoral College in the same amendment would be an added benefit.

Everything could change.

Numbers, Not Voters

Aside from outright attacks and procedural hurdles that suppress the vote and give Republicans an edge (more on those in the following chapters), there is another two-pronged attack in the Republicans' war to preserve minority rule in America.

The first prong is that a faction of Republicans wants to find a new answer to the broad question "Who deserves representation in the United States?"

This question is as old as the country, and it was even re-answered with the ratification of the 14th Amendment. As Senator Jacob Howard, R-Michigan, explained when he introduced the 14th Amendment, "The basis of representation should depend upon numbers. . . . Numbers, not voters; numbers, not property; this is the theory of the Constitution."

But this theory of the Constitution is being increasingly challenged by America's right wing.

In 2016, the Supreme Court heard *Evenwel v. Abbott*, wherein two Texas voters had sued the state of Texas in an attempt to overturn the constitutional principle that "every person deserves representation." As the *New York Times* reported in June 2019,

> *[the plaintiffs'] preferred method, shared by a number of conservative politicians, would erase from state political maps not only noncitizens, but also children—two groups that aren't evenly distributed across states. The resulting maps would tend to shift power from the places where children and noncitizens are more plentiful to places where there are more older and white residents. At the state level, such maps would also strip from these groups a principle as old as the Constitution: that even someone who cannot vote still deserves representation.*[64]

The Supreme Court ruled unanimously that the state could draw districts based on overall population—but the Court also left the door open as to whether states could *choose* to draw district maps based only on the *voting-age population*. In the words of the late Republican "redistricter par excellence" Thomas B. Hofeller, such maps in Texas "would be advantageous to Republicans and non-Hispanic whites."

Hofeller drew thousands of maps in his life—thousands of permutations of state maps drawn and redrawn to find all the ways that Republicans could gain electoral advantages without violating the letter of the Voting Rights Act. When he died, Republicans had no idea that he had saved those maps on hard drives. They also had no idea that Hofeller's daughter would discover those hard drives—and then turn them over to Common Cause, a government accountability group. When Common Cause went through his files, they found a trove of prepared maps for redistricting Republican-controlled states such as Texas and North Carolina.

The files, along with Hofeller's notes, serve as a smoking gun of the Republicans' concerted effort to draw new districts that nominally meet the criteria of the Voting Rights Act but functionally give "Republicans and non-Hispanic whites" an electoral advantage as a nationwide minority.

A key aspect of his plan was that Republican-controlled states would be allowed to count their population based on voting-age population instead of total population, because blacks and, particularly, Hispanics tend to have more children than whites at this time.

Stacey Abrams Was Robbed

The white men who run most of the elections in Georgia were never going to let a black woman become governor. Or, like their colleagues in Florida, any African American. But especially Stacey Abrams, a smart (Yale Law School) young woman of color who had been a highly effective legislator in the Georgia General Assembly.

There's history here. In 1867, a total of 33 black men were sent to the Georgia Constitutional Convention (to help write a new, post–Civil War, non-slave-state constitution for the state), where they promptly introduced provisions calling for free public school for black children, the right of black men to serve on juries overseeing cases involving white defendants, and doing away with debtors' prisons in the state. None made it into the constitution.

The following year, 32 black men were elected to that state's General Assembly, where they introduced legislation banning racial discrimination on public transportation, protecting black laborers from abuse, and ensuring "the protection of [black] citizens' rights."

Within a few months, the white men of Georgia's legislature had unseated their black colleagues, an event that reverberated all the way to Washington, DC, where unionist Republicans charged that this was proof that Georgia was still not politically reconstructed after the war.

In 1870, the US Congress allowed Georgia back into the Union, in part because Georgia's General Assembly passed two of the black members' bills, providing for nondiscrimination on public carriers and the creation of a public education system. Twenty-six black men were elected that year and allowed to serve.

But the black members of the Georgia legislature suffered terrible harassment, both from their colleagues and from members of the newly re-formed Ku Klux Klan, the nation's preeminent domestic terrorist group, which had begun an aggressive program of lynching, robbery, rape, and terror—particularly around election time—throughout the South. Only nine black men were elected in 1872, and within a decade the legislature was again entirely white.

Fast-forward to 2013. For three generations, the Voting Rights Act of 1965 had constrained Georgia's white politicians in their efforts to keep the state's power structures in white hands by preventing black people from voting. Every time they wanted to close a voting precinct in a black neighborhood or shorten black polling place hours, they'd had to submit the proposal to the US Justice Department for approval, which almost never was granted.

Every time they wanted to purge large numbers of black people from the voting rolls, they had to look over their shoulders at the Department of Justice (DOJ) and worry.

They couldn't introduce bizarre anti-voting laws like the "exact match" law that required a voter's registration card to exactly match his or her main form of ID, allowing polling station workers to disqualify voters—as they saw fit after checking out the color of the voter's skin—based on a period after their middle initial appearing on their ID but not their registration form, for example.

Republican Senator Brian Kemp of Georgia had introduced an exact match bill in 2008; it was shot down the next year by the DOJ as being discriminatory. But that was before 2013, when, in the case of *Shelby County v. Holder*, the Supreme Court eliminated the requirement that laws or rules like exact match had to be precleared by the DOJ before Georgia could put them in place.

Thus, when Kemp became secretary of state and was in charge of all voting in the state of Georgia, and the state no longer had to attend to the Voting Rights Act because of the *Shelby County* case, he reinstated exact match just in time for the 2018 election and used it to disqualify the registrations of more than 50,000 mostly black voters.

It was a decision that not only benefited pretty much every Republican in the state running for election or reelection in 2018, but also hugely benefited Kemp, who was Stacey Abrams's opponent in the gubernatorial race that year.

Race-based voter suppression has a long history in America. But the Republican response to the election of America's first black president was probably the most dramatic increase in these efforts in the lifetime of anybody alive today.

During the eight years that Barack Obama was president, seven of the 11 states with the largest black populations passed aggressive voter suppression laws. Nine of the 12 states with the largest Hispanic populations did the same. And nine of the 15 states that required preclearance under the Voting Rights Act passed, after the Supreme Court gutted that law, draconian voter suppression laws that principally affected people of color, college students, and people old enough to be on Social Security.[65]

States that had large black populations—like Georgia —even shut the polls the Sunday before Election Day on Tuesday, because black churches had been organizing very successful "souls to the polls" voting drives after church services. Georgia State Senator Fran Millar said that he and other Georgia Republicans were "investigating if there is any way to stop this [voting] action [by black people]" and that they "will try to eliminate this election law loophole [early voting on Sundays] in January."[66]

Election loophole? one might ask. As Wendy Weiser, who directs the Brennan Center for Justice's Democracy Program, wrote for the *American Prospect*, "An Ohio official, explaining his 2012 vote to limit early voting hours, said: 'I guess I really actually feel we shouldn't contort the voting process to accommodate the urban [read: African American] voter-turnout machine.'"[67]

Republican-controlled states across America passed hundreds of laws to make it harder for racial minorities, as well as young people and the elderly of all races, to vote, with the most severe passed in 2015 and 2016. The Brennan Center for Justice documented those states in which Republican legislative majorities made such changes just in 2016:

- In Montana, civil rights groups were banned by law from helping people cast absentee ballots.
- North Dakota passed a strict voter ID law.
- South Dakota made it much harder for ex-felons to get back their right to vote.
- Nebraska cut back days for early voting.
- Kansas required both proof of citizenship and government-issued photo ID.
- Alabama passed severe ID restrictions.

- Iowa restricted voter registration drives, passed a strict ID law, made early and absentee voting harder, and cut the voting rights of ex-felons.

- Wisconsin passed a strict ID law and limited early voting.

- Illinois curbed voter registration drives.

- Missouri passed a voter ID law.

- Indiana passed a law to institutionalize voter purges and restricted the kinds of ID that can be used.

- Ohio cut early voting and made it harder to cast an absentee or provisional ballot.

- West Virginia cut early voting from 17 days to 10 days.

- Virginia made it harder for groups to register people to vote and passed a draconian voter ID law.

- North and South Carolina both put voter ID restrictions in place.

- Georgia passed Brian Kemp's exact match voter registration law, as well as voter ID.

- Florida cut early voting, passed laws threatening to imprison people improperly running voter registration drives (causing the League of Women Voters to stop registering people in that state), and made it harder for ex-felons to recover their voting rights.

- Mississippi passed a voter ID law, as did Tennessee and Arkansas.

- Texas curbed voter registration drives and passed an ID law.

- Arizona limited mail-in ballots.

- Rhode Island passed an ID law, as did New Hampshire, that specifically made it much harder for college students to vote.[68]

- In 2019, in response to 2018 Democratic gains in Arizona, Kentucky, and Texas, as of this writing all three states have Republican-sponsored legislation in the pipeline for the 2020 election to make voting or registering voters harder. Techniques include making it a go-to-prison crime for making *any* mistakes on your voter registration form in Texas; Tennessee is similarly threatening people doing voter registration drives with prison if there are errors on the forms they turn in; and Arizona is making the entire voting process more complex.[69]

Meanwhile, Republicans were vigorously taking people's names off the voting rolls through a variety of purge methods.

The Brennan Center found that just between 2014 and 2016, in the two years leading up to the presidential election, over 14 million people were purged from voter rolls, largely in Republican-controlled states. Brian Kemp purged over a million in Georgia alone.

Calling the findings "disturbing," the Brennan Center noted, "Almost 4 million more names were purged from the rolls between 2014 and 2016 than between 2006 and 2008. This growth in the number of removed voters represented an increase of 33 percent—far outstripping growth in both total registered voters (18 percent) and total population (6 percent)."[70]

In the minority voting precincts that had been overseen by the DOJ back when the Supreme Court's *Shelby County* decision stopped the feds from looking over the shoulders of state officials in those places with a long history of race-based voter suppression, Republicans *totally* closed 868 polling places between the 2013 *Shelby County* decision and the 2016 election.[71] The result is that between the 2012 and 2016 elections, black voting participation fell nearly 7 percent.[72]

The story told by Republicans was that the drop came about because Hillary Clinton wasn't as popular as Obama and she wasn't black. But even in states and counties where black people were on the ballot, there was still a large drop in black voter participation. Although the Hispanic population in America is among the fastest-growing ethnicities, Latinx voters fell by .4 percent in 2016.

The only reasonable explanation is that the GOP's voter suppression efforts were successful.

In Georgia, they worked particularly well. Kemp had used several different voter suppression methods, from voter ID to massive voter purges to closing or time-limiting DMV offices that could issue IDs in black areas while extending their hours in white neighborhoods. He closed more than 200 polling places, mostly in poor and minority neighborhoods.[73]

Out of over 3.9 million votes cast in Georgia, Kemp won by a mere 55,000, about the same as the number of people he'd forbidden from voting because there wasn't an exact match of the middle names or initials or commas on mostly black voters' registration forms submitted in the months running up to the election.[74]

Not to mention over 1.5 million voters he'd removed from the rolls—such as Martin Luther King Jr.'s cousin, 92-year-old Christine Jordan, who was one of thousands turned away at the polls or given a provisional ballot that was never counted.[75] Jordan had been voting every two years at the same precinct for a full 50 years until Kemp's radical administration removed her name from the rolls.

Stacey Abrams ran a great race, and as Hillary Clinton later pointed out, she lost the election only because of voter suppression efforts by Brian Kemp and the GOP.[76]

Stacey Abrams's story isn't just a story about Georgia. It's the story of a political party that has lost touch with average American voters and has made the deliberate choice to hold power by a variety of forms of election manipulation and, in some cases, outright fraud.

The stakes are high: control of state and federal government. Meanwhile, the risks are low. Several people of color have been sent to prison for voting when they shouldn't (because they were ex-felons and didn't know about the law disenfranchising ex-felons), but the white Republicans who put into place and administer these modern-day Jim Crow systems are almost never prosecuted. Worse, they usually are well paid and rapidly climb the political ladder.

It all became necessary because the previous con job that the GOP had been running on the American electorate since the Nixon presidency stopped working toward the end of the Obama presidency. The following chapters examine some of the tactics that Republicans are still using to suppress, dilute, and otherwise steal Americans' votes.

Exit Polling around the World

Most Americans, when they hear the name Viktor Yush-chenko, vaguely remember a Ukrainian politician lying in a hospital bed with a severely disfigured face, the result of poisoning with a deadly form of dioxin, the toxic ingredient in Agent Orange. But it was exit polls that got him there.

Exit polls are polls taken outside of voting stations or polling places, where people who have already voted are questioned as they're leaving. They're considered far more accurate than other types of pre- or post-election polling because they don't rely on people answering their phones, returning a mailed inquiry, or asserting that they intend to vote when they may well not.

In a clean election environment, it's safe to assume that nearly 100 percent of the people polled actually voted, and history shows that such polls are typically (outside the United States) accurate to within a fraction of a point, or a point or two at most, depending on how many people are polled.

Exit polls are held in such regard that when, in the 2007 Kenyan election, Mwai Kibaki (the government's choice) was declared the election winner over Raila Odinga—who the exit polls reported had easily won—riots broke out, and, to quote the Carter Center, "more than 1,000 died and some 600,000 fled their homes."[77] In response, the Carter Center went to Kenya to monitor the re-vote (which was also severely marred by fraud).

Similarly, back in 2004 in Ukraine, Yushchenko—the reformer outsider candidate—was well ahead in the regular polling against Viktor Yanukovych. When the election returns came in, however, the government election commission reported that Yanukovych had won the election by 49.5 percent to 46.6 percent for Yushchenko. When it became widely known, however, that exit polling done by three different organizations concluded that voters had actually turned out for Yushchenko 54 percent to 43 percent for the guy the government said had won, people took to the streets in what was called the Orange Revolution.[78]

The *Washington Post* said in an editorial, "Despite the government's brazenly unfair campaign, a majority of Ukrainians voted for . . . Yushchenko [and] authorities then tried to steal the election."[79]

The US government, along with many European allies, declared outrage at the election fraud, proven by (among other events) the exit polls. They suggested that the election-result tampering was orchestrated by pro-Russian supporters of Yanukovych. To quell the riots, a new election was called, and as Yushchenko began to fall ill from the dioxin poisoning, he was elected the new president of Ukraine.

In Germany, exit polls have been used for years to functionally call elections as soon as the polls close, even though hand counting of paper ballots can take days. They're rarely off by more than a fraction of a single point. They're considered so reliable and so important that the German government criminalized releasing even preliminary results before the polls close; when two Twitter users leaked exit polls 90 minutes before the polls closed in 2009, it provoked a national scandal.[80]

Similarly, exit polls are routinely used to call elections all over the world, where paper ballots are almost universally used and thus can take days to count. A quick summary of AP headlines shows the reporting trend in the United States: "Exit polling indicates Peruvians vote to fight corruption,"[81] "Poland: Exit poll gives centrists edge in key mayoral races,"[82] "Exit polls suggest Irish voters have repealed abortion ban,"[83] "Exit polls: Dutch vote on spying law too close to call."[84] And that's just the Associated Press.

The British Broadcasting Corporation, a network sponsored by the government of Great Britain, where exit polls are also used to report election results before the paper ballots are counted, routinely uses exit polls all over the world to call elections.

A quick search finds elections being called by the BBC, in just the past three years, in Italy, the UK, Israel, Japan, India, the Netherlands, Haiti, Tunisia, France, Ireland, Bolivia, Bulgaria, Australia, Indonesia, Crimea, Portugal, Macedonia, Ecuador, the nation of Georgia, Kosovo, Latvia, Greece, Argentina, and even the Moscow mayor's race in Russia.[85]

Every single one turned out to accurately call the election it headlined.

Exit Polls in the US and Red Shift Explained

We used to use exit polls that way in the United States too. Techniques were tried and refined on a variety of local bases around the country for decades through the mid-20th century, but Warren Mitofsky fine-tuned it from an art into a science and conducted the first real acid test of the technique in 1967, accurately calling the Kentucky governor's race that year. Throughout the 1970s, virtually every election was called by the networks based on exit polls, and the technique was considered noncontroversial.

In the 1980 presidential election of Carter versus Reagan, the East Coast exit polling results were reported by NBC News hours before the West Coast polls had closed (the exit polls showed Reagan had won), producing bipartisan outrage; the networks promised to tighten up their handling of exit poll data, which was virtual news gold.[86]

Everything was going well until the 2000 election, when the exit polls clearly showed Al Gore winning the presidency (including in Florida, which, it turns out, he did win when all the ballots were counted by the news organizations a year after the election), and the networks called the election for Gore before all the states had reported their counts.

While election exit polls are still the gold standard worldwide, since that 2000 election they seem to have gone to hell in the United States.

In the 2004 presidential election, exit polls called John Kerry the clear winner with a margin of more than two million votes, even winning handily in Ohio, but this time the networks held back.

As ABC News reported in a postmortem of their reporting on the exit polling of the 2004 election,

> *The exit poll estimates in the 2004 general election overstated John Kerry's share of the vote nationally and in many states. There were 26 states in which the estimates produced by the exit poll data overstated the vote for John Kerry by more than one standard error, and there were four states in which the exit poll estimates overstated the vote for George W. Bush by more than one standard error. The inaccuracies in the exit poll estimates were not due to the sample selection of the polling locations at which the exit polls were conducted. We have not discovered any systematic problem in how the exit poll data were collected and processed.*[87]

The exit polling companies, in the four years since 2000, had developed a new strategy to report their polls—unique to the United States in its widespread use—in which they'd "adjust" their results to reflect what the individual states reported as the actual vote.

ABC News' postmortem noted, "[T]he final exit poll data used for analysis in 2004 was adjusted to match the actual vote returns by geographic region within each state."[88] That "final" and "adjusted" data purported to show that John Kerry had won by only about a half-million votes, and he'd lost the decisive state of Ohio, which became the reporting the networks went with.[89]

In 2004, fully 22 states experienced what has now come to be called "red shift"—where the polls are "wrong" but almost always in a way that benefits Republicans.

For example, in the 2016 election, the exit polls showed Hillary Clinton carrying Florida by 47.7 percent to Trump's 46.4 percent, although the "actual" counted vote had Trump winning by 49.0 percent to 47.8 percent. Trump gained 2.5 percentage points . . . somehow.[90]

In North Carolina, exit polls showed Clinton winning 48.6 percent to 46.5 percent, but the votes that were counted turned out with Trump's 49.9 to Clinton's 46.1, a red shift of 5.9 percentage points for the GOP.[91]

Pennsylvania's exit polls showed that Clinton won 50.5 percent to Trump's 46.1 percent, but when "eligible" votes were counted, Trump carried the state 48.8 percent to Clinton's 47.6 percent—a red shift of 5.6 percentage points.

In Wisconsin, it was Clinton beating Trump in the exit polls 48.2 percent to 44.3 percent, but the "real" count put Trump over the top at 48.8 percent to 47.6 percent, a red shift of 5.1 percentage points.

Perhaps even more interesting, in states without a Republican secretary of state, there is virtually no shift at all, either red or blue, and hasn't been *ever*. The election results typically comport with the exit polls in those states.

Given that red shift began to explode across the American electoral landscape in a big way with the 2000 election, and it continues to favor the candidates of one party in a way not seen in any other developed nation that does exit polling, a number of theories have evolved to explain it.

Warren Mitofsky, who'd been doing exit polling since the 1960s and invented the modern technique in the 1970s, found himself and his firm terribly embarrassed with the results of the 2000, 2002, and 2004 elections when the red shift numbers were enough to throw critical elections to Republicans. He came up with the theory of the "shy Republican voter," which postulated that, for some reason, Republican voters were just simply embarrassed to tell exit pollsters that they'd voted for a Republican.

That theory was widely reported in the media and became the go-to excuse for adjusting exit poll numbers by changing them to conform to state-reported results after the 2004 election.

Few people buy it, however, particularly since there are no similar examples in any other nation in the world, even where a winning leader may otherwise be seen as a war criminal or buffoon. Exit polls—except when there's clear fraud—are the single most accurate way to measure an election outside of counting actual ballots.

Voting Machines, Hacking, and Red Shift

Given that much of the red shift that America has seen in the past three decades exploded after the passage in 2002 of the Help America Vote Act (HAVA), which allocated billions of dollars to the states to buy electronic voting machines from private corporate vendors, many people alarmed by widespread red shift were quick to blame the machines.

And, indeed, they are easy targets.

The 2002 senatorial election in Georgia, done entirely on electronic voting machines that produced no paper or receipts, was severely marred by accounts of lost memory cards containing votes from largely urban areas and produced a result that flipped the polls upside down.

War hero Max Cleland, who'd left three limbs in Vietnam and was nationally famous and popular (and ahead in the Georgia polls by five points a week before the election), was defeated by eight points by Saxby Chambliss, a Vietnam War–era draft dodger who'd run a bizarre campaign questioning Cleland's patriotism.[92]

The Georgia governor's race that year saw a similar reversal of poll versus outcome results favoring the Republican challenger, Sonny Perdue, who was seven points down in the polls but beat incumbent Democrat Roy Barnes with a 16 percent swing on Election Day, something unheard of in modern politics absent a last-minute scandal (and there was none).[93]

Similarly, in the 2018 Georgia election, the Republican lieutenant governor candidate, Geoff Duncan, beat Democrat Sarah Riggs by 123,172 votes. Inexplicably, the Georgia electronic voting machines—which still don't have any audit ability or paper trail—registered slightly over 160,000 voters who simply chose *not* to vote for *either* of the lieutenant governor candidates. When Politico investigated, "the Georgia Secretary of State's office did not respond to repeated requests for comment."[94]

And when a lawsuit was filed against Secretary of State Brian Kemp (who both ran the election and ran successfully against Stacey Abrams for governor) to access the actual votes, a server was mysteriously wiped clean in a way that prevented even the NSA from recovering its data.[95]

Frank Bajak reported for the AP, "A computer server crucial to a lawsuit against Georgia election officials was quietly wiped clean by its custodians just after the suit was filed, the Associated Press has learned." Bajak said, "It's not clear who ordered the server's data irretrievably erased." The lack of data effectively killed the lawsuit, and when the AP repeatedly inquired of the agency that wiped the server, "It did not respond to the AP's question on who ordered the action."[96]

Howard Dean rather famously hacked into a Diebold election computer tabulator and changed the results of an election in 90 seconds on CNBC while filling in for Tina Brown on her *Topic A* show on August 8, 2004. When he was made chairman of the Democratic National Committee, the video was pretty much scrubbed off the internet, although recuts of it pop up from time to time.[97,98]

There was also, to add flames to the conspiracy fire, the simple reality that the two biggest voting machine vendors in the 2000s were banking giant Diebold, whose CEO, Wally O'Dell, famously wrote a leaked 2004 letter promising to "deliver Ohio for George W. Bush," and Election Systems & Software, which was started by two Christian end-times-rapture-believer brothers and then passed through other GOP-connected hands over the years.[99]

Hacker conventions, year after year, have featured demonstrations of how easy it is to hack a wide variety of voting machines used in the United States—in 2018, the hack of a clone of the Florida election system was accomplished in less than 10 minutes by an 11-year-old.[100]

It's an example of why Ireland, after experimenting with American voting machines for one election, sold its $80 million worth of machines for scrap metal (for a mere $79,000); it refused to resell them as voting machines, taking a huge loss on the deal, so that there was no chance any other country would buy them and make the mistake of using them in an election.[101]

As the *New York Times* has documented, among others, our intelligence services are worried about how easily foreign governments (particularly Russia, China, and North Korea) can get into most states' election systems.[102] The states themselves, however (at least those controlled by Republicans; California famously decertified all of its machines in 2004), continue to stonewall or refuse to change to more secure systems.[103]

And while it's not hard to believe that in a state with a centuries-old tradition of election fraud (mostly by white people against black people) like Georgia, "losing" memory cards with votes on them[104] or even "patching" machines in the weeks before the election without notifying anybody (both things that are well documented)[105] could have thrown an election, it's harder to conceive of it as a multi-decade national conspiracy.

On the other hand, voter suppression very much has been at the core of a multi-decade effort by the GOP and may well explain red shift as much as hacked or rigged machines. We'll circle back to that in a moment.

Privatizing the Vote with Voting Machines

While the security of our elections has apparently been put at considerable risk by bringing private, for-profit vendors into the voting business, there's a larger issue that virtually nobody is discussing.

The Bush administration's practice of hiring Dick Cheney's nearly bankrupt company, Halliburton, with multibillion-dollar no-bid noncompetitive contracts to replace functions carried out by GIs for over 200 years (at a fraction of the cost) might have saved Halliburton and made millions for Cheney and his family but was only a "small" crime against our commons, which include our military. Such privatization of our military functions has led to nearly half of the defense budget now going to for-profit corporations.

Similarly, privatizing Chicago's parking meters by leasing them to a European company and leasing Indiana's highways to an Australian corporation are crimes against the commons and our democracy, but small crimes.[106,107] Ditto for privatizing our schools, water systems, and electrical grids—activities that, since the 1980s, have gobbled up around half of all the electric and water utilities and, in Betsy DeVos's Michigan, about half of the schools.

Privatizing our prisons and immigration detention facilities leads to the perverse result of for-profit corporations lobbying for longer sentences for drug and other crimes, but that's a matter of public policy that can and should be debated in the open.

Privatizing our airwaves, as Bill Clinton's 1996 Telecommunications Act largely did, has turned out to be a public policy disaster and led to, as *Forbes* explained in a recent headline, the "15 Billionaires [Who] Own America's News Media Companies,"[108] but it's reversible with enough public outrage.

But the vote is the single mechanism by which we, the people, can register our approval or disapproval of such policies and even effect their reversal. It's the ultimate expression of the commons of our government, because it's how we determine the course and future of our government.

To have allowed privatization of the vote—as happened on a nationwide scale with HAVA in 2002—is a crime against democracy and our commons unlike any in the history of our nation.

Now our votes are counted in secret by private corporations with specific agendas that are met, in part, by spending millions on lobbying members of Congress. They refuse to show us their software, citing trade secrets, and generally lease, rather than sell, their generally Windows-based and deeply insecure systems to states.

At the very least, states should *own* any voting machinery and infrastructure used in their territory, and the software should be open-source. At best, we should follow Ireland's example.

Suppressing the Vote with Provisional Ballots

The Help America Vote Act may provide another answer to the puzzling mystery of American red shift.

That legislation, written in large part by Representative Bob Ney, R-Ohio, contains a provision requiring people who show up to vote—even if they've been purged from the voting lists—to be given something called a "provisional ballot."

"The main reason we did that," the former congressman told me, "was because, particularly across the Deep South, people were simply being turned away at the polls. In most cases it was because they were black, but in many cases it was also being done in districts where the opposition party controlled most of the election apparatus, typically Republicans turning away people in Democratic districts.

"We wanted to make sure," he added, "that every eligible voter had both a chance to vote and some level of certainty that his or her vote would be counted after they went to all the trouble of voting."

The parable about the road to hell being paved with good intentions is worthy of citing here. The HAVA law was passed on a bipartisan basis, after the hanging-chad disaster in Florida in the 2000 election was the main excuse given the media for that state's substantial red shift. But the giant loophole it created for GOP vote suppressors was that provisional ballots are almost never counted.

Rules vary from state to state, but usually if voters are given a provisional ballot, they must then, within a few days of the election, present themselves in person at a state or county office to prove that they are who they say they are and that they were legally registered to vote and were purged incorrectly. The HAVA law requires that voters getting provisional ballots be told this, but in actual practice in Republican-controlled states this is almost never the case. (Although, even when it is, the percentage of people who'd be willing or able to take time off work to jump through all these hoops is tiny.)

Independent investigative reporter Greg Palast, whose work is published by the BBC, the *Guardian*, *Rolling Stone*, and Salon, found this to be very much the case (and worse) when he accompanied Martin Luther King Jr.'s 92-year-old cousin, Christine Jordan, to the polls in Georgia, and poll workers repeatedly refused to give her even a provisional ballot until Palast intervened.[109]

After voting for half a century in the same place, she'd been purged from the rolls by Secretary of State and gubernatorial candidate Brian Kemp's policies and people. Eventually, after multiple tries with Palast threatening lawsuits and making a scene on camera at the polling place, Jordan got a provisional ballot, although it almost certainly was never counted.

In the years immediately preceding the election, Kemp had purged well over a million voters from Georgia's rolls and prevented the registration of around 50,000 mostly African American voters from being processed. In all probability, large numbers of these people turned out and voted anyway, with provisional ballots. And, not realizing that their provisional ballot vote would never actually be counted, if they encountered an exit-poll taker outside the polling place, they probably would have registered their vote with the pollster.

Thus, one simple explanation for all that red shift in Republican-controlled swing states is that the voters reporting their Democratic votes to exit pollsters simply didn't know that their vote would never be counted, and neither did the pollsters.

None of these issues are part of the mainstream of public debate in America, although they've been hot topics in other countries, from Australia to Ireland to Canada. Perhaps if enough of us speak out, one day soon our election exit polls will again agree with our vote tabulations.

Diluting the Vote with Gerrymandering

Gerrymandering and money in politics are the two main ways in which the impact of our votes—after they're cast and counted—is diminished, often to the point of irrelevance. American voters are aware of these, and their persistence and power may well account for why so many people don't bother to register to vote, and only a fraction of those registered show up on any given election day.

Gerrymandering entails using the process of redrawing congressional districts to provide a substantial political advantage to one party at the expense of others. A gerrymander of state legislative districts in Wisconsin in 2012, for example, produced a map where Republicans lost the statewide vote for the members of the State Assembly by 47 percent to 53 percent, but the GOP nonetheless ended up with 60 seats in the 99-seat legislative body.

In 2017, Emily Bazelon of the *New York Times* reported the results of a Brennan Center study:

> *In the 17 states where Republicans drew the maps this decade—for 40 percent of the total House seats in the country—their candidates won about 53 percent of the vote and 72 percent of the seats. In the six states where Democrats drew the lines, for only about 10 percent of the House, their candidates won about 56 percent of the vote and 71 percent of the seats.*[110]

Gerrymandering has been part of American politics since one of the founders, Elbridge Gerry, supervised, as governor, the redrawing of Massachusetts's congressional maps to benefit his Democratic-Republican Party in the election of 1812. Both parties have done it since that era, although the Supreme Court, in a 1964 ruling, decreed that districts must at least have roughly equivalent population numbers.

On June 27, 2019, the Supreme Court ruled that while "racial" gerrymandering is still unconstitutional, it's just fine for political parties to do "partisan gerrymandering."[111]

Six Democratic-controlled states use nonpartisan commissions to draw congressional lines, a practice that has made elections more competitive and interesting in New Jersey and California. Thirteen states do the same for state legislative districts.

In every case, experience shows that nonpartisan districts produce results that more accurately reflect the makeup of the voter base, but now that the Supreme Court has told the GOP that they can gerrymander to their hearts' content, it's a safe bet that they'll simply use political rather than racial considerations as their justification, and their billionaire friends will be dropping hundreds of millions of dollars into the 2020 and 2030 state elections to ensure GOP control of the state legislatures that redraw district lines.

By going for nonpartisan commissions, the Democrats, assuming that the Supreme Court would limit partisan gerrymandering, essentially unilaterally disarmed. Time will tell whether they adopt Republican policies or if we'll continue to see more and more states severely gerrymandered by the GOP as they did in North Carolina, for example: in 2018, a state that votes pretty much 50/50 Democratic/Republican sent three Democrats and 10 Republicans to the US House of Representatives.[112]

Depressing the Vote with Money in Politics

Money in politics has a long and ignominious history.

Corruption by money of individual politicians, and of the legislative process as a whole, hit three peaks in the history of our nation: during the Gilded Age of the late 1800s, the Roaring Twenties in the last century, and the years since 2010 when the Supreme Court struck down numerous campaign finance and good-government laws, throwing the doors open to corporate and billionaire cash with its *Citizens United* decision.

The Gilded Age excesses led to the Tillman Act of 1907, which made it a federal felony for a corporation to donate money or anything of value to a campaign for federal office. It was gutted by *Citizens United*.

The political corruption of the Harding, Coolidge, and Hoover administrations led directly to the great crash of 1929, causing most corporations to pull back from the political arena until the 1970s, when Lewis Powell revived it with his infamous memo to billionaires and corporate CEOs.

After the Watergate investigations revealed Nixon's bribery and other scandals, Congress passed numerous reforms of money in politics, although the Supreme Court struck down the most consequential of them; and as long as there's a conservative majority of at least five votes on the Court, that's unlikely to change.

Therefore, this is the situation today:

- A billionaire oligarch, Rupert Murdoch, programs his very own television news network to promote the interests of the billionaire class with such effectiveness that average working people are repeating billionaire-helpful memes like "cut regulations," "shrink government," and "cut taxes"— policies that will cause more working people and their children to get sick and/or die; will transfer more money and power from we, the people, to a few oligarchs; and will lower working-class wages over time.[113]

- A small group of billionaires have funneled so much money into our political sphere that "normal" Republicans like former US senators Jeff Flake and Bob Corker point out that they couldn't get elected in today's environment because they'd face primary challengers funded by right-wing billionaires.

- The corporate media (including online media), heavily influenced by the roughly $1 billion that the Koch network, Sheldon Adelson, the Mercers, etc., poured through their advertising coffers and into their profits in the last presidential election, won't even mention in their "news" reporting that billionaire oligarchs are mainly calling the tunes in American politics, particularly in the GOP.

- Former president Jimmy Carter pointed out on my radio show that the United States "is now an oligarchy, with unlimited political bribery," in part as a result of the right-wing Supreme Court decision in *Citizens United*.[114]

- Nobody in corporate media—even on the "corporate left"—is willing to explicitly point out how billionaires and the companies that made them rich control and define the boundaries of "acceptable" political debate in our country.

- Thus, there's no honest discussion in American media of why the GOP denies climate change (to profit petro-billionaires), no discussion of the daily damage being done to our consumer and workplace protections, and no discussion of the horrors being inflicted on our public lands and environment by GOP appointees.

- There's not even a discussion of the major issue animating American politics just one century ago: corporate mergers and how they damage small business and small towns.

Although it's been this way before in American history, it wasn't within our lifetimes. The last time the morbidly rich had this much power in American politics was in the 1920s, when an orgy of tax cutting and deregulation of banking led to the Republican Great Depression.

Our nation now faces a massive crisis provoked by the loss of democratic representation for the majority of the American electorate. Neither party today does much of anything for the bottom 90 percent of Americans,[115] as so clearly demonstrated by a 2014 study out of Princeton showing that the likelihood of legislation passing that represented the interests of that bottom 90 percent was equivalent, statistically, to white noise.[116]

The predictable—and tragic for our republic—result is massive voter apathy and a loss of voter engagement.

The Beginnings of a Myth: Voting Fraud

For over a century, most states used biometrics to verify voter identity. Signatures done in front of a witness are nearly impossible to fake (unlike IDs, which can be easily faked). Polling place workers would compare the original registration signature with the signature of the person signing in to vote, and if they didn't match, the worker would disqualify the voter.

When the Motor Voter Act was passed in 1993, not a single state required proof of citizenship to vote, and there was no national problem of voter fraud. The threat of a few years in jail is more than enough to discourage even the most ardent partisan from trying to double-vote or fraudulently vote.

If somebody wanted to travel internationally, he or she got a passport; the purpose of a driver's license prior to 2006 was merely to make sure that incompetent people weren't moving 3,000 pounds of steel at 60 miles per hour across the nation's roads, and to be able to track down and hold to account people who abused the privilege.

With passage of Motor Voter in 1993, though, the "Illegals will now be registered to vote!" screech immediately came bubbling up from the throats of Republican consultants and politicians.

The *Washington Post* reflected the newspaper's position in a 1995 editorial:

*A group of Republican governors that includes Califor-
nia's Pete Wilson, who has already sued to have the law
overturned, objects ... that it [the Motor Voter law] is also
a ploy by Democrats to strengthen the party's electoral
chances, since many of those whom easier registration might
add to the voter pool are groups inclined to vote against the
GOP; and ... that the law could facilitate voter fraud.*

The editors of the *Post* added dryly, "As for fraud, registration at motor vehicle offices and by mail already works fine
in many parts of the country, including in the District [of
Columbia].... The governors ought to reconsider."[117]

But the torch had been lit, and a quiet movement began
within the GOP to sound the alarm, fueled by Motor Voter,
that there could be millions upon millions of noncitizens who
were or soon would be registered voters. And if those millions
of "illegal aliens"—a perennial Republican boogeyman—
were to turn out at the polls, particularly those brown people
from south of the border, they'd flip the nation into the hands
of the Democrats.

Voting Fraud: From Myth to Dogma

Bush and Cheney came into the White House shaken and
widely viewed by the American electorate as having marginal
legitimacy; they certainly couldn't even claim a mandate to
govern, after having lost the popular vote.

Karl Rove helped organize publicity about the "crisis" of
"illegal voting" as a possible explanation for Bush's losing the

popular vote by a half-million, and Attorney General John Ashcroft launched the 2002 Ballot Access and Voting Integrity Initiative in the Justice Department, requiring all 100 US federal prosecutors to "coordinate with local officials" to combat the scourge of illegal voting and bring to justice the millions of presumed malefactors who made the election so close.[118]

Over the next three years, at a cost of millions of dollars, and after examining tens of millions of voters and more than a billion votes, Ashcroft was able to document and successfully prosecute only 24 people nationwide for voting illegally—and *none* of them had committed in-person voter fraud of the kind that would be stopped by voter ID. (Most were people double voting, and the majority of those were wealthy white Republicans who had homes in two states and voted in person in one and mailed in a ballot to the other state; such folks got a fine, typically around $2,500. There were also a few felons who voted and didn't know it was illegal.)

Karl Rove put on the pressure; they *had* to find a few people (ideally black or brown people with fake IDs) who could be made into national examples of the evils of in-person voter fraud, if they were ever to convince Americans that stronger ID laws were necessary to stop noncitizens from voting.

So the Bush White House demanded that all 100 of the nation's federal prosecutors—all Bush appointees—move investigating voter fraud to the front of their agendas, sidelining other federal crimes. Eight of the prosecutors objected and were summarily fired.

In Washington state, prosecutor John McKay was fired because he refused to intervene in the 2004 election with fraud charges when Republican Dino Rossi lost that state's governor's race by a mere 129 votes. McKay told the *Seattle Times* that after a thorough investigation by his office, "there was no evidence, and I am not going to drag innocent people in front of a grand jury."[119] That was a career ender.

In New Mexico, prosecutor David Iglesias resisted GOP pressure to create a show trial around two teenage boys who somehow got onto the voting rolls even though they were both under 18 and *neither* had voted. In a 2007 op-ed in the *New York Times* titled "Why I Was Fired," he wrote, "What the critics, who don't have any experience as prosecutors, have asserted is reprehensible—namely that I should have proceeded without having proof beyond a reasonable doubt. The public has a right to believe that prosecution decisions are made on legal, not political, grounds."[120]

The firings were a major scandal in the Bush administration, although time has faded the public recollection of them.

But the GOP was just getting started. By the end of 2004, 12 states had passed laws requiring ID to vote.

Coincidentally, a comprehensive study by the Eagleton Institute of Politics at Rutgers University found that, overall, requiring ID to register to vote reduced the registered voting population in the states that did so by around 10 percent. In the 2004 election, "Hispanic voters were 10 percent less likely to vote in non-photo-identification states compared to states where voters only had to give their name." Among African Americans, they found that the "probability of voting was 5.7 percent lower for Black respondents in states that required non-photo identification."[121] Requiring photo ID raised it into the 10 percent region.

Even the vote of Asian Americans, another group more inclined to vote Democratic than Republican, was suppressed by around 8.5 percent by the ID requirement.[122]

Again, none of these nonvoters were ever found to be non-citizens; it's just that among these populations there were larger numbers of people who lived in cities where they didn't need a driver's license because they didn't own a car, or were too poor to own a car, and thus lacked the picture ID required by the new state laws. Among white people, the effect was to suppress the vote of college students, the working poor, and retired people.

The story of how voter ID laws suppress minority and poor people's votes hadn't yet hit the news in a big way, but it was electrifying Republican politicians and consultants. And their billionaire donors.

The American Legislative Exchange Council (ALEC) is a nationwide nonprofit that brings together Republican state legislators and lobbyists to consider mostly lobbyist-written legislation for the Republican state senators and representatives to take back home and introduce. (Democrat Mark Pocan, when he was a Wisconsin state representative, registered for an ALEC meeting in that state and attended it. He called in to my radio show as they were throwing him out of the place, once they'd figured out he wasn't a Republican. "It was pretty bizarre," he told me.) Via the largely Koch-funded ALEC, the GOP distributed what ALEC refers to as "model legislation" (in fact, they're prewritten laws that are often submitted by legislators verbatim) that would make it harder for minorities to vote, including requiring ID—and proof of citizenship—to register to vote, along with repeated requirements to show ID at the time of voting. Willing Republican state legislators added their own twists to the model legislation offered by ALEC by, for example, increasing penalties for voter fraud.

As reporter Ari Berman wrote for *Rolling Stone* in 2011,

> *In Texas, under emergency legislation passed by the GOP-dominated legislature and signed by Gov. Rick Perry, a concealed-weapon permit is considered an acceptable ID but a student ID is not. Republicans in Wisconsin, meanwhile, mandated that students can only vote if their IDs include a current address, birth date, signature and two-year expiration date—requirements that no college or university ID in the state currently meets. As a result, 242,000 students in Wisconsin may lack the documentation required to vote next year.*[123]

State by state, Republicans were making it harder for young people, poor people, low-income working people, minorities, and retired people to vote. But the issue still hadn't caught on nationally.

Then came Kris Kobach.

Kris Kobach: The Voting Fraud Myth Becomes a Mission

Kris Kobach's national debut was as a speaker on the first day of the 2004 Republican National Convention in New York City. I attended that convention and broadcast my show from there, sitting next to Sean Hannity, interviewing and meeting many of the GOP luminaries. And most of what they wanted to talk about was the same as Kobach's speech: the danger of Mexicans sneaking into the United States and voting (along with robbing, raping, and drug running).

Ironically, they didn't seem so concerned with Mexicans taking American jobs. When I repeatedly brought up with Republicans how Ronald Reagan had pretty much stopped prosecuting employers after his 1986 amnesty for five million "illegals," and how entire industries that used to have an all-American labor force and were heavily unionized, like construction and meat packing, were now mostly just employing people who were in the country illegally, they'd just shrug their shoulders. One said, "Well, it did help break the unions" or words to that effect.

Kobach, though, was soon to turn his warnings about brown-skinned people from south of the border into a lucrative legal and consulting business, helping cities and townships draft anti-illegal-immigrant laws. In most cases, the laws were quickly overturned in the courts, and the cities ended up with huge legal bills, both for Kobach's services and for defending themselves after they promulgated his laws.

ProPublica did an investigation into it all, published in 2018 with the title "Kris Kobach's Lucrative Trail of Courtroom Defeats." It reads, in part,

> *The towns—some with budgets in the single-digit-millions—ran up hefty legal costs after hiring him to defend similar ordinances [to one he helped pass in Missouri]. Farmers Branch, Texas, wound up owing $7 million in*

legal bills. Hazleton, Penn., took on debt to pay $1.4 million and eventually had to file for a state bailout. In Fremont, Neb., the city raised property taxes to pay for Kobach's services. None of the towns are currently enforcing the laws he helped craft.[124]

University of Missouri law professor Larry Dessem told ProPublica that Kobach reminded him of the character Harold Hill in *The Music Man*. "Got a problem here in River City," he said, "and we can solve it if you buy the band instruments from me. He is selling something that goes well beyond legal services."[125]

Kobach has turned stopping Mexicans from voting (a nonexistent problem in the United States) into a mini-industry, at times arguing that there were more than 18,000 "illegals" registered to vote and/or voting in Kansas (when he became secretary of state, he was unable to find even *one* of them), and at other times echoing Donald Trump's assertion that the number nationwide was about the same as the margin of Trump's popular-vote loss to Clinton—in the neighborhood of three million.

In fact, more people are struck by lightning in any given month than try to vote without being a citizen in any given year; numbers nationwide from credible sources place it between a few dozen and perhaps a hundred nationwide in any given national election. A study published in the journal *Election Studies* in 2014 suggests that the number may have been far fewer than even 100 people—nationwide—and almost all voted in error or by mistake, or didn't understand voting law.[126]

And double voting is just as rare.

There is *no* credible evidence of the "busloads" of Hispanic or black people going from polling place to polling place to repeatedly vote, cited by Donald Trump, by former Maine governor Paul LePage, and repeatedly on Fox News and other sources, even existing anywhere in the United States at any time in our lifetimes.

When the ACLU took Kobach to court for trying to enforce a punishing strict-photo-ID law in Kansas that he'd helped get passed, the judge essentially ridiculed his claims of noncitizen voters after Kobach's best witnesses (including Hans von Spakovsky of the Heritage Foundation) not only were unable to document their own claims but repeatedly had their previous claims called out accurately as lies. Kobach lost the case.

But Kobach still pushes for large voter purges.

Interstate Crosscheck and the Election Integrity Scam

The Republicans have successfully pushed their monstrous lie of double voting and noncitizen voting because of the ways that states handle voter registration rolls. Ideally, a state's voter registration rolls should carry only the names of people who are both currently legal residents of the state and qualified to vote. The reality is much different.

For example, I grew up in Michigan and voted in that state until I was 27 years old, in 1978. That year, we moved to New Hampshire, where I registered to vote—and never told Michigan that I'd left. Five years later, we moved to Georgia, where

I registered to vote and did so for more than a decade—again, not telling either Michigan or New Hampshire that I'd moved out of state. In 1997, we moved to Vermont, where I again registered to vote. In 2005, we moved to Oregon, and the same story. In 2010, we moved to Washington, DC, then back to Oregon in late 2017.

Most states remove a person from the rolls only if the person doesn't vote for at least a few presidential elections in a row or if the person has notified the state that he or she has moved (a rarity), and therefore only occasionally update their voter rolls. Thus, odds are that my name would have been found on the rolls of two or maybe even three or four states over the years, registered to vote in every one of them.

I never voted in two states at once. And outside of the dozen or so people a year who do so nationwide, mostly in error, neither does anybody else.

But it's easy enough for a partisan like Kobach to point to duplicate voter registrations in multiple states as "proof!!" of double voting. He and Trump (and most of the right-wing media) constantly cite figures of people registered in multiple states—something that is *not* a crime in any state—as if those people were in fact double voting, which is a crime.

Kobach helped put together and promote an elaborate scheme called Interstate Crosscheck to catch these "double voters." By comparing names of registered voters in one state against rolls in multiple other states, he was able to identify millions of people who, like me, were still registered to vote in more than one state. Again, no crime and no double voting—but a heck of a sound bite for Fox News.

Kobach compiled huge lists of "duplicate" voters for one red state after another, with hundreds of thousands of names on each list. Republican secretaries of state enthusiastically purged the "duplicate" names from their rolls. As Republican strategist Paul Weyrich admitted in 1980, "Our leverage in the elections quite candidly goes up as the voting populace goes down."[127]

But there was an added benefit for Kobach and the GOP: many (and perhaps most) of the people "caught" by Crosscheck weren't people like me who move a lot. They were, instead, people who had identical or similar names.

White people came to America from wildly diverse places speaking dozens of different languages, from northern Russia to southern Italy, from the British Isles to Serbia to deep within India. They brought with them a huge diversity of names.

On the other hand, Asians, Hispanics, and African Americans tend to have much smaller name pools. African American slaves were often named after their owners, and because most of the slave states were settled by a relatively nondiverse population of white people, their name pool is smaller than that of whites. Ditto for Hispanics, who acquired their names from the Spanish conquerors, representing a single-country name pool. And Asians draw from a relatively small pool of names to begin with.

Thus, when running Crosscheck, the "duplicate" names—particularly within a state—tend to disproportionately belong to people of color, which accounts for why voting purges in places like Georgia leading up to 2018 bit so hard into the pool of registered African American and Hispanic voters.

Because of these problems, select states have stopped using Kobach's program, but others are still purging away and will continue to as long as there is no actual right to vote codified in either our law or our Constitution.

Kobach took his system with him to the White House, where Donald Trump appointed him in May 2017 with much fanfare to his Presidential Advisory Commission on Election Integrity—charged with *proving* that double voting and in-person voter fraud were rampant nationwide.

Unable to find any proof of these charges anywhere in the United States, though, just as had happened a bit more than a decade earlier when George W. Bush was firing federal prosecutors for not being able to locate these malefactors, the commission dissolved, by executive order, on January 3, 2018, with almost no mention in the media and nary a tweet from Trump, who continues to maintain that three million people voted illegally in 2016.[128]

PART THREE

Solutions

The Electoral College is a disaster for a democracy.
—Donald J. Trump

If they don't give you a seat at the table, bring a folding chair.
—Shirley Chisholm, America's first black woman elected to US Congress

The GOP's Grand Stand
against Voting and Democracy

The idea of democracy is simple: issues are put to voters, each person gets one vote, and whatever position gets the most votes becomes law.

Our country was not established as a direct democracy, though, and citizens aren't given an affirmative right to vote in the US Constitution; the issue is placed in the hands of our "laboratories of democracy," the states.

When people think of voting, they tend to think of the presidential election every four years. Many people don't pay attention to local elections, and more and more Americans have found the political landscape so divisive that they've simply tuned out.

According to Pew, in a survey conducted in early 2016 of largely eligible but unregistered voters, when asked why they didn't vote, 30 percent responded, "My one vote isn't going to affect how things turn out"; 35 percent responded, "Voting has little to do with the way real decisions are made."[1] These attitudes indicate that our democracy is facing a real crisis of legitimacy and that expanding and improving our democracy is more critical now than ever, if we are to wrest control of our government from the hands of corporations and billionaires.

This is a crisis of legitimacy for our nation, and even worse is that many Americans are tuning out simply because they see that our government is unresponsive to the desires of the majority of the American people.

As Columbia law professor Tim Wu pointed out in the *New York Times* in March 2019, "The defining political fact of our time is not polarization. It's the inability of even large bipartisan majorities to get what they want on issues [that concern them]. Call it the oppression of the supermajority. Ignoring what most of the country wants—as much as demagogy and political divisiveness—is what is making the public so angry."[2]

This is a key problem in our country right now. It's not that Americans don't agree on many issues; it's that Americans have no way of achieving the policies they agree on.

Republicans Oppose "For the People Act of 2019"

March 8, 2019, was a chilly day in Washington, DC, and a big vote loomed in the House of Representatives. Speaker Nancy Pelosi addressed a group of lawmakers, staffers, and citizens on the steps of the Capitol; the crowd was bundled up to keep warm, waving American flags and holding posters in support of the forthcoming vote.

In the lead-up to the vote, Republicans made it clear that they would have no part in a bill that would, among other sweeping reforms, extend the vote to formerly incarcerated citizens.

For example, Representative David McKinley, R-West Virginia, trotted out the idea that expanding democracy is wasteful spending and asked on Facebook, "Do you want your tax dollars going to bankroll campaigns? H.R. 1 provides a 6:1 government match for 'small' campaign contributions. This would put taxpayers on the hook for attack ads, robocalls, and targeted ads on social media for candidates."[3]

Republicans in the House suggested several amendments, including one that, as Fox reported, would have condemned "illegal immigrant voting."[4]

Later in the day, the House of Representatives passed H.R. 1, the For the People Act of 2019, along partisan lines, 234–193. The bill's summary states simply that it is "to expand Americans' access to the ballot box, reduce the influence of big money in politics, and strengthen the ethics rules for public servants, and for other purposes."

The headline on Fox's website summed up the Republican position once the bill passed: "House Dems pass 'power grab' voting rights bill; McConnell says proposal has no chance in Senate."[5]

It's telling, but not surprising, that Republicans are painting H.R. 1 as a power grab by Democrats. As covered in part 2, Republicans have opposed expanding the vote for more than a century for various reasons and through various mechanisms (and Democrats did largely before 1965).

As Representative Zoe Lofgren, D-California, said at the time, Democrats and pro-democracy advocates see the bill differently: that it "grabs power away from the elites and the power brokers and gives it to the people."[6] That's the predictable outcome of any bill that expands voting rights and attempts to cap the corrupting influence of money in politics—and that's what has the Republicans scared.

Looking at the proposals in H.R. 1, it's clear why Republicans are nervous: it would roll back more than a century of right-wing voter suppression efforts, and it would extend and improve our democracy, threatening the oligarchs' current stranglehold on policy making in the United States.

The bill introduces a combination of sweeping changes and minor tweaks, and it's broken into three distinct but deeply connected sections:

1. Voting
2. Campaign Finance
3. Ethics

At its core, democracy is a simple system in which we, the people, send signals to our government, which in turn implements policy, laws, and large-scale projects on behalf of us. In this system, elections are the occasions when we, the people, go to our polling places, where we can send signals to our government by submitting our votes.

In an ideal system, every citizen is an eligible voter, and every eligible voter can go to his or her polling place at every election, and then his or her vote is perfectly counted.

In real elections, there are system failures at every step of the way:

1. Not every citizen is registered to vote.
2. Republican-controlled states have made it difficult to register to vote through mechanisms like mandating citizenship IDs and then closing DMVs in majority black areas (as Republicans did in Alabama in 2015).[7]
3. Even if a citizen thinks he or she is registered to vote, many Republican-controlled states actively purge inactive voters.

4. Elections are held on weekdays, and many workers may not be able to take time off to vote.

5. Polling places are not always convenient to get to, and staffing issues can cause long waits and lines. If lines are particularly long and the weather is particularly nasty, many voters may choose either to not take time off work or to simply stay home.

6. Because of issues with "miscalibrated" privately owned voting machines or confusing ballots or outright vote stuffing, our votes are not always accurately counted.

7. Because of the corrupting influence of money in politics and our media, and the resulting amount of misinformation that is directed at voters, even if every step of the voting process were safe, secure, and easy to use, voters might still not be all that well informed about their choices when casting their ballot.

It may languish and die in the Republican-controlled Senate, but the For the People Act of 2019 marks a good first step toward addressing many of these issues.

Automatic Voter Registration

The bill would create automatic voter registration at the national level, which would thwart many of the state-level voter suppression tactics exploited by Republicans over the last half-century of elections.

As the Brennan Center for Justice notes, automatic voter registration does two things. First, it makes registering to vote an opt-out choice rather than an opt-in choice. This might seem like just a semantic change, but significant research shows that individuals are more likely to participate in a program that is opt-out rather than opt-in.

A 2013 Association for Psychological Science blog post describes how this logic explains why the United States has fewer registered organ donors than other countries:

> In the United States, 85 percent of Americans say they approve of organ donation, but only 28 percent give their consent to be donors by signing a donor card. The difference means that far more Americans die awaiting transplants. But psychologists Eric J. Johnson, a professor at Columbia University Business School, and Daniel Goldstein, formerly at Yahoo and now a principal researcher at Microsoft Research, found in a 2003 study that in many European countries, individuals are automatically organ donors unless they opt not to be—organ donation is the default choice. In most of these countries, fewer than 1 percent of citizens opt out. In an article published in Science in 2003, Johnson and Goldstein theorized that opting out in those countries was simply too much of a hassle for most people, since it involved "filling out forms, making phone calls, and sending mail."[8]

The very same logic may help to explain why so many Americans are not registered to vote. In a 2017 Pew survey, 27 percent of eligible but unregistered voters said that they "intend to register but haven't done so yet."[9]

This is not the same as compulsory voting, as citizens are still able to opt out of voter registration, but it makes being registered to vote the default position for American adults. (Compulsory voting addresses a different failure in the ideal democratic system: the problem of people not showing up to their polling place or casting a ballot at all, even if they are registered.)

The second thing that automatic national voter registration would accomplish is that it would create a system whereby voting agencies keep electronic voter information that can be transferred to election officials, instead of paper registration forms that could be misplaced or lost by local election officials looking to skew the vote.

Sweden has automatic voter registration and a database that tracks every citizen's name, address, birth, and marital status. At every election, the government sends proof of registration material to every Swedish citizen who is in the national voting database.

While this system may provoke cries of "government over-reach!" from libertarian and survivalist types, it would ensure that partisan state officials could not tamper with the voter rolls without also justifying changing the national voter rolls.

With automatic national voter registration in place, Jim Crow voter suppression efforts would have been rendered null, and Schwerner, Goodman, and Chaney never would have been murdered while registering black voters around Philadelphia, Mississippi.

Through much of the 20th century, automatic voter registration would have been a cumbersome, file-intensive program on a larger scale than even Social Security. (Social Security was such a large program, literally, that there was no building big enough in Washington, DC, to store the paper, filing cabinets, and equipment that the program's bookkeeping required.)

Today, all of the necessary information for automatic national voter registration could be easily collected and stored electronically on secure government servers, and there's little reason not to.

Right now, 15 states and Washington, DC, have approved automatic voter registration with very promising results for democracy. The Brennan Center declared in 2018 that "the results have been exciting. Since Oregon became the first state in the nation to implement AVR in 2016, the Beaver State has seen registration rates quadruple at DMV offices. In the first six months after AVR was implemented in Vermont on New Year's Day 2017, registration rates jumped 62 percent when compared to the first half of 2016."[10]

Restore the Vote for Returning Citizens

Grant Ferguson, a blue-eyed, clean-shaven sales manager in Iowa, was taken aback when a sheriff's deputy arrived with a warrant for his arrest.

Even more shocking was the reason why. According to an AP report, Ferguson "was stunned when he learned the reason: his unsuccessful attempt to vote in the 2016 election. The supporter of President Donald Trump would ultimately face $5,000 in legal costs to resolve the charges, which stemmed from a bureaucratic error that unknowingly kept him on

Iowa's list of ineligible felon voters." Iowa is unforgiving when it comes to ex-felons casting ballots, the report said, and prosecutors pursue cases relentlessly:

> *A Clinton [Iowa] man who is disabled from a brain injury was prosecuted after he mistakenly believed poll workers would alert him if there was a problem with his voting eligibility. A low-income Muscatine man who cast a provisional ballot after disputing that he was ineligible still owes $2,300 in court costs. The mayor of tiny Moorhead was forced to resign and prosecuted for illegally voting after a judge revoked his deferred judgment in a drug case.*
>
> *Prosecutors pursued cases even when ex-offenders such as Ferguson believed they were legal voters but cast provisional ballots so that their eligibility could be determined later.*[11]

In many of these cases, the ex-felons did not intend to break the law, and they may have even been trying to hedge their bets by casting a provisional ballot because they were unsure whether they were eligible to vote (as in Ferguson's case). Sometimes the state's felon list isn't updated, or local precincts haven't checked the state's list for updates, causing errors in who is allowed to vote.

Some states, following the lead of Jeb Bush in Florida's 2000 election, use these mistakes to purge the voter rolls of convicted felons *and anyone who shares a similar name* with a convicted felon. In the case of Kris Kobach's Crosscheck crusade against nonexistent voter fraud, secretaries of state have purged individuals from the rolls even when they had a middle initial that was different from a convicted felon's and regardless of whether the two individuals had different Social Security numbers.

As covered earlier, in many states—such as Texas and Florida—individuals with criminal records are disproportionately black or Hispanic, and the Republican Party has been very successful in making sure that they can't vote. In Florida, a swing state, fully 21 percent of African American men can't vote (as of 2018) because of a felony conviction.[12]

The For the People Act of 2019 goes a step beyond automatic voter registration when an individual turns 18—it would also require states to automatically register ex-felons when their sentence is complete, upon release. Right now, 12 states (five in the South) ban automatic voter restoration once felons have completed their sentence.

Senate Majority Leader Mitch McConnell, R-Kentucky, has called the bill "a solution in search of a problem"—but in the cases of Grant Ferguson and dozens of others in Iowa, automatic restoration of voting rights would have saved them an arrest, lost wages, time in court, and a hefty fine.

For Americans like Grant Ferguson—who has served his time and is seeking to participate in American democracy—the problem of voter suppression and inconsistent local and federal laws have costly consequences.

Once a citizen has served his or her time for a crime and is deemed rehabilitated to reintegrate into society, it should be considered essential to reintegration that that citizen be able to participate in our democracy and exercise his or her right to vote.

Certainly, if a citizen has committed no crime aside from having a name similar to that of a criminal, it is a major problem if he or she is purged from the voter rolls, as happened in Florida in 2000.

Taking it a step further, Bernie Sanders pointed out during a town hall in May 2019 that Vermont is one of two states in the union (Maine is the other) that lets felons vote while in jail. While the idea of such a thing going national quickly became an object of ridicule, the most important point is lost.

We say that we think of felons as human beings whom we are working to redeem and reintegrate into society. What better way to reintegrate a person into society than giving the person a choice in selecting his or her representatives and sometimes even voting on ballot measures that may become law?

End Voter Caging

In the lead-up to the 2018 midterms, the *Economist* ran an article that clearly laid out how the Supreme Court's 2013 ruling in *Shelby County v. Holder* gutted the preclearance provision of the 1965 Voting Rights Act, and how states took that to mean that it was open season to purge state voter rolls. The article quotes research from the Brennan Center for Justice that found that "nearly 16m voters were removed from the rolls between 2014 and 2016. That is almost 4m more than were purged between 2006 and 2008. The increased purging far exceeds population growth or the growing number of registered voters."[13]

This is a system failure that automatic voter registration would not necessarily fix. Theoretically, a voter could be registered nationally but purged from the rolls for local and state elections. Since local and state elections are where most of the decisions that affect people are made, this represents a potentially serious failure of democracy.

Voter caging is just one form of voter suppression, but as the Brennan Center's figures show, it is also very effective. Here's how it works: State officials claim that they are simply seeking out people who may have died or moved out of state, so that they can be removed from the rolls for accuracy's sake. Under the pretense of rooting out those ineligible folks, election officials send out mass *nonforwardable* direct mailings to every registered voter. If any mail is returned because a voter moved (even if he or she just moved down the street), election officials use that as a reason to formally challenge the person's right to vote.

The For the People Act of 2019 outright bans the practice unless the challenger gives an oath that he or she has a "good faith factual basis to believe the person is ineligible to vote or register to vote."[14]

Voter caging puts the burden of proof on the citizen to prove that he or she has a right to vote. This provision in H.R. 1, combined with automatic voter registration, flips the script and puts the burden of proof on state officials to prove that a citizen should lose his or her right to vote.

With just these two provisions (ending voter caging and implementing automatic voter registration), millions of Americans would gain the right to vote, and that right to vote would be protected from frivolous attempts to take it away. But it doesn't guarantee that voters would have the time or means to make it to the polls on Election Day.

Make Election Day a National Holiday

If the United States can get every eligible citizen registered to vote for a given election, the next hurdle is to make sure that voters are able to go to a polling place and actually cast a ballot.

Fully 14 percent of registered voters who did not vote in the 2016 election reported that they were too busy or had a conflicted schedule, with another 12 percent reporting that they had an illness or disability, and another 8 percent reporting that they were out of town or away from home, according to a Pew Research Center analysis of Census Bureau data in 2017.[15]

The US Constitution doesn't specify when elections are to be held. Until 1845, each state was able to set its own date for elections. Before 1845, states held elections in the 34 days before the electors in the Electoral College voted.

In 1792, the presidential election was held from Friday, November 2, until Wednesday, December 5, in a system that resembled our current presidential primary system. While the system gave voters plenty of time to cast their votes for the popular vote, it also created a system whereby states that cast their votes earlier could influence the decisions of voters who cast their ballots later. (This problem also exists in our partisan primary system, and states jockey to hold their primaries and caucuses earlier to give their voters outsized influence.)

In 1845, President John Tyler signed an act by Congress that made the general election uniform throughout the country. From 1845 forward, Election Day was officially the first Tuesday after the first Monday in November.

While it may seem arbitrary to today's Americans, Congress calculated that the first Tuesday was when most American voters would be able to make it to the polls. Jane C. Hu explained the logic in a *Quartz* article, writing that Congress in 1845 assumed a few things to be true about American voters at the time, aside from knowing that voters would be tax-paying white men in good standing with their respective state governments:

1. Voters were mostly farmers who would likely be done with harvest by November but would still need to take their harvest to town markets (normally held on Wednesdays).
2. Most voters wouldn't be able to travel on Sunday, the Christian Sabbath, for religious reasons.
3. Many Christian voters would be celebrating All Saints' Day on November 1.[16]

None of these considerations are relevant today; it's time to make Election Day a national holiday.[17,18]

Vote by Mail

Voting by mail offers a tidy solution for voters who are unable—because of either physical or time constraints—to vote in person at a polling place. Voting by mail has also been thoroughly tested at the state and local levels across the United States, and 22 states have provisions for certain elections to be held *entirely* by mail-in ballots.

The way it works is simple, as the National Conference of State Legislatures (NCSL) explains: "All registered voters receive a ballot in the mail. The voter marks the ballot, puts it in a secrecy envelope or sleeve and then into a separate mailing envelope, signs an affidavit on the exterior of the mailing envelope, and returns the package via mail or by dropping it off."[19]

In many ways, vote by mail reflects the United States' original election system up until 1844, when voters cast ballots over the period of a month.

Oregon, Colorado, and Washington distribute all their ballots by mail, but it is not the exclusive way that ballots are cast—and many people still want the sensation of actually delivering their ballot to a physical location, rather than having a stranger pick it up from their mailbox.

Researchers at the MIT Election Data + Science Lab found that "73 percent of voters in Colorado, 59 percent in Oregon and 65 percent in Washington returned their ballots to some physical location such as a drop box or local election office. Even among those who returned their ballots by mail in these states, 47 percent dropped off their ballot at a U.S. Post Office or neighborhood mailbox rather than having their own postal worker pick it up at home."[20] This is critical, because the goal in our democracy ought to be to *provide as many opportunities as possible for people to vote*.

Vote by mail is very well tested, with proven results in terms of boosting voter turnout in both rural and urban areas, particularly in off-cycle elections.

A rural Nebraska county of about 2,000 people recently experimented with conducting its entire May 15 primary by mail. Every voter in Garden County, Nebraska, was mailed a ballot, and they had to return it by mail or to a drop box by the end of May 15. Remarkably, Garden County saw a 58.7 percent voter turnout in the 2018 primary—*more than double* the Nebraska-wide average of 24.3 percent.[21]

In April 2018, Anchorage, Alaska, held its first vote-by-mail election for a local election, and it received about 80,000 votes out of 218,000 registered voters—up from the record 71,000 votes that had been cast in 2012.[22]

In addition to increasing voter turnout and making it easier to vote, vote by mail nullifies the need for absentee voting, as every voter is given the opportunity to vote absentee, by mail.

But vote by mail also has its shortcomings. As the NCSL notes, "Mail delivery is not uniform across the nation. Native Americans on reservations may in particular have difficulty with all-mail elections. Many do not have street addresses, and their P.O. boxes may be shared. Literacy can be an issue for some voters, as well. Election materials are often written at a college level."[23]

Lawmakers can solve some of this by pushing to have the state governments pay for postage, as Governor Kate Brown is currently promoting in Oregon. In Washington and California, prepaid mail ballots are already the norm.

Vote by mail, if implemented correctly, could go a long way toward boosting voter turnout in federal elections. However, there's plenty more we can do to ensure that every eligible citizen has the right and ability to vote, such as providing staffed vote centers, now used in Denver and the entire state of California, offering help to voters with disabilities, language translations, and other assistance. The savings of replacing local polling places with vote by mail can be put toward vote centers that provide early voting and well-trained staff to assist voters who need it.

Extend Early Voting

Vote by mail can overcome the physical hurdle of getting voters to polling places, but we can also make polling places more available to voters than just during polling hours on a Tuesday in November.

Extending early voting helps to address the time constraints that voters in the real world face. Real voters have families, children, jobs, and other pressing demands that make it difficult to drop everything on a Tuesday in November to stand in line potentially for hours. Even after standing in line for hours, many legitimate voters have been told they are not properly registered and offered a provisional ballot to cast—which *may or may not* be counted.

Extending early voting would help workers and caregivers find time to get to the polls—and, importantly, expanding early voting would reduce the length of lines at polling places on Election Day, not only making it easier for voters to choose a day and time that worked for them, but also giving voters the confidence that voting would be a relatively quick process because of shorter lines.

Unlike other initiatives to expand the vote and to make it easier to vote, extending early voting enjoys overwhelming bipartisan support. The Brennan Center for Justice reported in 2016,

*One recent poll found 75 percent of likely voters support
early voting, with 60 percent expressing "strong" support.
A 2013 poll of North Carolina voters found 85 percent
of respondents back early voting, including more than
75 percent of Republicans. Americans also oppose efforts
to restrict early voting—an October 2014 poll found only
11 percent of voters supported reducing early voting before
Election Day.*[24]

The Brennan Center recommends that every state offer early voting beginning "a minimum of two full weeks before Election Day, including weekend and evening hours."[25]

Paper Ballots or Paper Receipts

Back in 2002, polling showed popular Georgia Democratic Senator Max Cleland with a solid, five-point lead over his Republican challenger, Saxby Chambliss, a week before Election Day. But when the votes were counted using electronic voting machines made and operated by a private, for-profit corporation, Chambliss emerged victorious.

So what happened? Well, it might have had something to do with a software patch that Diebold installed in machines in Democratic-leaning counties months before voters went to the polls.[26] But we'll never actually know what happened. As Robert F. Kennedy Jr. noted in his piece on the 2002 Georgia Senate race, "It is impossible to know whether the machines were rigged to alter the election in Georgia: Diebold's machines provided no paper trail, making a recount impossible."[27]

That's the whole problem with electronic voting machines: we'll never really know. Private companies don't have to reveal their software secrets because they are protected under copyright law. And again, unlike with paper ballots, you can't see when someone messes with your touchscreen vote. It happens outside of plain sight.

Ultimately, however, the biggest problem with electronic voting machines is that they violate the core principles of our republic.

As Truthout reported, "Ireland and Canada tried out electronic voting machines and eventually abandoned them."[28]

There is a movement to allow voting through an online portal or by email, which would perhaps be even less secure. These methods are subject to malicious code that can be automated, such as through denial-of-service attacks on servers or through malware.

Voters also could be fooled by "spoof sites" that looked like official voting portals but weren't. Just as a common election trick is to mail voters cards telling them to show up in the wrong precinct or on the wrong date, emailing them the wrong link in an official-looking email would be child's play.

Even if the vote wasn't altered, voters' data and metadata could be harvested by middlemen who could use or sell it. As far back as 2013, blatant issues with "e-voting" were already becoming clear in developing countries, and many developed countries and regions were already abandoning it.[29]

Even the US ambassador to the United Nations from 2017 to 2018, Nikki Haley, called for a return to paper ballots—at least in the Congo. The *Washington Post* reported in September

2018 that "Haley called on Congo to abandon its plan to use the machines for the first time in favor of paper ballots—what she called a 'trusted, tested, transparent and easy-to-use voting method.'" And earlier that year, she said, in her official capacity, "These elections must be held by paper ballots so there is no question by the Congolese people about the results. The U.S. has no appetite to support an electronic voting system."[30]

Just two months after the *Washington Post* published that story, 25 states in the United States allowed voting by email or online portals, and around 350,000 voting machines were in use in the 2018 midterm elections.

What's good for elections in the Congo would be good for elections in the United States: the best solution to the vulnerabilities of old electronic voting machines and e-voting is to do away with them completely and return to 100 percent paper ballots. Short of that, electronic voting machines should be owned by the government and programmed with open-source software.

Stopping Politicians from Choosing Their Own Voters

As noted earlier, the Supreme Court in 2019 threw open the door to political gerrymandering by whichever party can gain control of a state in an election year ending in 0 (the Constitution requires a census and reapportionment every decade). Legislation should be passed explicitly overturning this decision and providing for "good government" nonpartisan commissions to draw legislative districts.

The Electoral College and a National Popular Vote

The last two Republican presidents have both lost the popular vote (2000, 2016). But they won the electoral vote and thus became president.

The *Washington Post* reported shortly after the 2016 presidential election that Wyoming has three electoral votes and a population of 586,107, while California has 55 electoral votes and 39,144,818 residents. If electoral votes are distributed evenly among each state's residents, individual votes from Wyoming carry 3.6 times more weight than those from California.[31]

On March 15, 2019, Colorado governor Jared Polis, a Democrat, signed a bill that made Colorado the 12th state (and 13th jurisdiction, including Washington, DC) to join an interstate compact to pledge the state's elector to the winner of the national popular vote.

As conservative commentator Matt Vespa pointed out on the website Townhall, "Prior to this move by Colorado, 11 states totaling 165 votes agreed to this compact. Now, it's 12 states with 181 electoral votes. Nothing is triggered unless this push cobbles together enough states that will grant the winner 270 votes."

The compact is just 89 electoral votes shy of rendering the Electoral College null and void; because it takes only 270 votes to win the Electoral College, if states representing 270 electors sign on to the compact, then the national popular vote becomes decisive because those 270 pledged electors make up a majority.

Many people wrongly believe that pledging the Electoral College to a national popular vote is a partisan solution that would only help Democrats—especially with Paul LePage making declarations about the plan like "White people will not have anything to say. It's only going to be the minorities who would elect."[32]

In reality, it would end the concept of battleground states because every voter's vote—wherever he or she lives—would count the same as every other voter's.[33] Indeed, in 1969 a bipartisan constitutional amendment to abolish the Electoral College passed the House of Representatives 339 to 70, far more than the two-thirds necessary in either house of Congress to pass a constitutional amendment.

While voters in swing states might protest that the national popular vote would hurt them by minimizing their voices, that is only because right now they have a disproportionately large impact on our elections and how presidential candidates campaign, even as early as the during the parties' primaries.

The national popular vote would neutralize the Electoral College without rewriting the US Constitution. That would go a long way toward ensuring that our presidents are elected by the majority of Americans.

Voting Systems Shape Elections: Getting beyond Two Parties

In United States elections, even if we abolished the Electoral College (or functionally abolished it), we would still likely have partisan gridlock. This is because the United States operates under a "first past the post, winner takes all" electoral system. This almost always produces a two-party system, where even basic governmental functions like passing a budget become partisan gauntlets.

It's as close to a law in political science as there is—Duverger's law, which says simply that systems that use first-past-the-post elections will end up with two parties, either because smaller parties lose support and "die" until only two remain or because smaller parties converge into larger parties until only two remain.[34]

Even though there are more than 30 nationally registered political parties in the United States, only the Republican and Democratic parties ever have a real showing, with secondary parties rarely garnering more than 5 percent of the popular vote, except in historically exceptional circumstances.

In first-past-the-post voting, a voter casts one vote per position, and whoever gets the most votes for that position wins. It has the advantage of being simple. But it also creates a system in which two parties dominate.

Combined with the partisan primary system, it also often forces voters into choosing the "least bad" candidate who is least offensive to everyone, instead of choosing the candidate whom a voter most strongly supports based on his or her positions on pertinent issues.

A ranked-choice, or instant-runoff, voting system addresses this. Ranked-choice voting also makes it impossible for a candidate to win without winning the support of a majority of voters.

The way it works is simple: instead of casting a single vote for a single candidate, each voter gets to rank the candidates, listing his or her first choice, second choice, etc. In the first round, only the voters' first choices are counted. If one candidate wins a simple majority in the first round, that's that. If no one wins outright in the first round, then the candidates who finish last are eliminated. When those candidates are eliminated in the second round, their voters still get a voice, because their second choices are counted. This cycle repeats until there are only two candidates left, at which point the candidate with the most votes (which would then be a majority) wins.

Ranked-choice voting reduces the power of money in politics, because so much of it is used for negative campaigning, which becomes less effective in such a system. It also creates an elected political field that more accurately reflects the electorate, by giving voters a wider array of choices. Ranked-choice voting is already in place in cities and for certain elections in places around the country, and it's gaining popularity quickly.

While ranked-choice voting would be most transformative in federal and state elections, it could have a tremendous impact on our politics if the Democratic and Republican parties adopted ranked-choice voting for primaries, particularly for the presidential primaries. In fact, Democrats in Alaska and Hawaii will do so in 2020.

Compulsory Voting

Voting is mandatory in Australia and Belgium—so why not here?

Many people would loudly proclaim that compulsory voting is an anti-democratic idea, but it seems unlikely that anyone would argue that Australia and Belgium are dictatorships because they fine people who don't vote. The $20 fine is high enough to make it worthwhile for voters to participate but low enough that it is unlikely to bankrupt someone or be burdensome to enforce.

Australia implemented compulsory voting in 1924; the voter turnout in Australia has never been lower than 91 percent.[35]

Emilee Chapman, a political scientist at Stanford University, describes the simple logic behind compulsory voting: "It really offers this society-wide message: There is no such thing as a political class in a democracy. Voting is something that is for everybody, including and especially people at the margins of society."[36]

While compulsory voting will probably never pass in America, there are ways to encourage people to vote that are legal and would probably withstand a constitutional challenge, from the persuasive (nationally funded campaigns like those done to promote savings bonds and victory gardens during World War II) to the direct (tax deductions available only to voters). It's a great companion discussion to the national debate about automatic voter registration.

We have compulsory jury duty, draft registration, and taxes. Voting is part of being a citizen, the price we pay for living in a democracy.

DC and Puerto Rico Statehood, Splitting Up Big States

It's a mass of irony for all the world to see;
it's the nation's capital, it's Washington, DC.

—Gil Scott Heron

The Democratic Party is facing a crisis that it's experienced only once before in its history: the near-complete loss, for multiple generations, of control of the Senate—and thus the loss of any say in the makeup of the federal judiciary, including the Supreme Court. Within the next two decades, half of the population of the United States will live in just eight states and be represented by only 16 (out of 100) senators.[37] Right now, about two-thirds of the US population lives in just 15 states, represented by only 30 senators (and thus 30 percent of the Senate).

There's history here, and Democrats need to learn from it fast.

Generally speaking, as the country was adding new states (mostly in the 19th century), the population of a territory that wanted to become a state had to hit the threshold necessary for a single representative in the House of Representatives, which, in 1864, was 125,000 residents. Nonetheless, in 1864 during the Civil War, Abraham Lincoln and his Republican Party (which controlled both the House and Senate at the time) brought the Nevada territory into the Union—all 7,000 residents living in Nevada. Had Nevada waited until it had enough residents to qualify for a single House seat, it wouldn't have been admitted as a state until 1970.

But Nevada added two Republican senators, giving the GOP solid control over the Senate. In 1876, to solidify that majority, Republican president Ulysses S. Grant and his party granted Colorado—with 40,000 residents—statehood.

Republicans doubled down on the process in 1889, when they'd just ousted Democrat Grover Cleveland from the White House, and Republican president Benjamin Harrison not only admitted the Dakota Territory into the union but split it in two to produce four senators and two representatives for the GOP. (North Dakota had 36,000 residents in 1880;[38] South Dakota had 98,000.[39])

In roughly 40 years the GOP added eight senators, largely cementing their control of the Senate until the Great Depression; from Lincoln's inauguration in 1861 until 1933, Democrats controlled the Senate for only eight years.

Democrats need to consider doing the same. There are two ways: add new states and split up some of the existing states.

Almost half of our states have fewer than four million people,[40] with 14 of them having fewer than two million, and generally the least populous states are the most rural and the most reliably Republican.

California, with about 40 million residents, could—given these numbers—split itself into 10 or more states, adding 18 or more senators (not all but most Democratic). New York, with 20 million, could easily become two (New York City and the rest of the state) or even four if the boroughs of NYC were broken out.

There is virtually no discussion of this among Democrats; it's time to start a conversation.

Similarly, at the very least, the District of Columbia should become a state *now*.

"Taxation without representation" is proudly displayed on license plates of vehicles registered in Washington, DC. Ironic, considering that the city is the capital of a nation that was birthed in the colonial cries of "No taxation without representation!"

Though residents in Washington, DC, pay federal taxes and the District has more citizens than either Wyoming or Vermont,[41] DC is not a state, has no votes in Congress, and has had only three Electoral College votes since the 1961 passage of the 23rd Amendment.

Puerto Rico is in a similar situation, although residents of the territory do not generally pay federal taxes. In a 2017 referendum, 97 percent of the island's residents voted in favor of statehood.[42]

The people of both Puerto Rico and Washington, DC, want the places where they live to become states, and Republicans are terrified at the prospect because both places are overwhelmingly Democratic, which would add four Democratic senators, producing a Senate that more accurately reflected the overall American electorate.

Until Puerto Rico and Washington, DC, are admitted as states into the United States, their respective nonstate statuses mean that their residents are facing a systemic form of voter suppression.

Get Out There, Get Active

Some readers may despair, seeing the figures in this book and learning how billionaires and the Republicans have disenfranchised millions. Although the solutions here have focused on fundamental ways that we can restore the vote and strengthen our democracy, most change happens locally.

Individuals can help every step of the way—from asking neighbors whether they are registered to driving neighbors to the polls and acting as a poll watcher.

The situation will not change without Americans participating. No individual politician will change the trend toward oligarchy. The seeds for change in American politics are scattered in towns, boroughs, and counties across the country.

The power of money in politics diminishes as Americans create more local people-powered coalitions to exert positive pressure for popular local issues. As one of the first campaign ads for Representative Alexandria Ocasio-Cortez, D-New York, declared, "They've got money, we've got people."

Finally

The truly exceptional part of American exceptionalism is that our country was birthed not in genetics or national identity but out of the egalitarian ideals of the Enlightenment. Imperfectly implemented and acted out as those principles have been, particularly in our first hundred years, we've moved over the centuries toward a better and better expression of them.

The past 40 years or so have seen backward movement in the ability of our government to respond to the desires of most Americans, while that same majority is outspoken about wanting more transparent, more accountable, and more representative governance.

Our voting system is a product of some of the best ideas of the 18th century. In the 21st century, we have in our hands the ability to bring it more fully in line with the Lockean and Jeffersonian ideals and create "a more perfect union."

Tag, you're it.

NOTES

Introduction: The Heartbeat of Democracy

1. Thomas Paine, "Dissertation on First Principles of Government," *The Greatest Works of Thomas Paine: 39 Books in One Edition* (Musaicum Books, e-book).
2. http://reclaimdemocracy.org/powell_memo_lewis/
3. https://www.nbcnews.com/politics/politics-news/states-removed-17-million-voters-rolls-two-years-government-agency-n1023416
4. https://www.csmonitor.com/Commentary/Global-Viewpoint/2013/0305/Argo-helps-Iran-s-dictatorship-harms-democracy
5. http://news.bbc.co.uk/2/hi/events/newsnight/1174115.stm
6. https://www.nytimes.com/2017/09/25/us/wisconsin-voters.html
7. https://www.thenation.com/article/the-gops-attack-on-voting-rights-was-the-most-under-covered-story-of-2016/
8. https://www.gregpalast.com/why-are-greg-palast-and-jesse-jackson-suing-kris-kobach/
9. https://founders.archives.gov/documents/Adams/06-04-02-0091
10. Paine, "Dissertation on First Principles of Government."

Part One: The Hidden History of the Vote in America

1. http://www.delamar.org/gnpwitch.htm and https://symonsez.wordpress.com/tag/1787-constitutional-convention-weather/
2. https://oll.libertyfund.org/pages/1787-madison-s-notes-of-debates-in-the-federal-convention
3. https://theintercept.com/2019/03/23/black-identity-extremist-fbi-domestic-terrorism/
4. https://www.nytimes.com/2018/11/03/magazine/FBI-charlottesville-white-nationalism-far-right.html
5. https://constitutioncenter.org/blog/hot-hot-hot-the-summer-of-1787/
6. https://www.cia.gov/library/readingroom/docs/DOC_0000872649.pdf
7. https://founders.archives.gov/documents/Jefferson/01-30-02-0451
8. John Ferling, *A Leap in the Dark: The Struggle to Create the American Republic* (New York: Oxford University Press, 2003), 425.
9. https://avalon.law.yale.edu/18th_century/fed68.asp
10. http://www.crf-usa.org/bill-of-rights-in-action/bria-25-2-the-major-debates-at-the-constitutional-convention.html
11. http://time.com/4558510/electoral-college-history-slavery/
12. https://www.washingtonpost.com/news/the-fix/wp/2016/11/09/getting-rid-of-the-electoral-college-dream-on-democrats/
13. Ibid.

14. https://www.washingtonpost.com/news/politics/wp/2017/11/28/by-2040-two-thirds-of-americans-will-be-represented-by-30-percent-of-the-senate/?utm_term=.685e1ec228bc

15. Letter from Abigail Adams to John Adams, March 31–April 5, 1776 (electronic edition), *Adams Family Papers: An Electronic Archive.* Massachusetts Historical Society, http://www.masshist.org/digitaladams/.

16. Letter from John Adams to Abigail Adams, April 14, 1776 (electronic edition), *Adams Family Papers: An Electronic Archive*, Massachusetts Historical Society, http://www.masshist.org/digitaladams/.

17. Susan B. Anthony, November 12, 1872, letter to an unknown correspondent, https://rbscp.lib.rochester.edu/exhibits/show/womens-rights-movement/anthony-and-stanton.

18. https://www.law.cornell.edu/supremecourt/text/83/130

19. https://now.org/resource/voter-suppression-targets-women-youth-and-communities-of-color-issue-advisory-part-one/

20. http://www.msnbc.com/msnbc/the-war-voting-war-women

21. https://time.com/5442434/north-dakota-voting-law-native-american-activism/

22. https://digitalcommons.macalester.edu/cgi/viewcontent.cgi?article=1146&context=tapestries

23. https://www.brennancenter.org/blog/state-native-american-voting-rights

24. https://oll.libertyfund.org/pages/1787-madison-s-notes-of-debates-in-the-federal-convention

25. https://vindicatingthefounders.com/library/madison-remarks.html

26. https://founders.archives.gov/documents/Jefferson/01-11-02-0047

27. http://www.let.rug.nl/usa/presidents/thomas-jefferson/letters-of-thomas-jefferson/jefl246.php

Part Two: The Economic Royalists' Modern War on Voting

1. http://armored-column.com/did-the-democrats-gop-switch-sides-after-the-voting-rights-act-in-1964/

2. https://www.theguardian.com/commentisfree/2013/aug/28/republicans-party-of-civil-rights

3. Bill Moyers, *Moyers on America: A Journalist and His Times* (New York: Anchor Books, 2005, reprint edition), 197.

4. https://www.clarionledger.com/story/news/politics/2016/07/26/trump-neshoba-fair-geoff-pender/87561270/

5. https://www.naacpldf.org/ldf-celebrates-60th-anniversary-brown-v-board-education/southern-manifesto-massive-resistance-brown/

6. Ibid.

7. https://www.thenation.com/article/brown-v-board-education-didnt-end-segregation-big-government-did/

8. https://www.nytimes.com/2007/06/29/washington/29scotus.html

9. https://www.epi.org/publication/brown-at-60-why-have-we-been-so-disappointed-what-have-we-learned/

10. https://www.rawstory.com/2019/02/trump-loving-ex-governor-says-electoral-college-needed-stop-minorities-picking-presidents/

11. https://www.gotquestions.org/calvinism.html

12. https://oll.libertyfund.org/pages/spencer-proper-sphere-of-government-1843

13. https://www.britannica.com/biography/Francis-Galton

14. http://eugenicsarchive.ca/discover/connections/5233dc9e5c2ec500000000c5#!

15. https://www.uvm.edu/~lkaelber/eugenics/

16. https://historynewsnetwork.org/article/1796

17. http://www.washingtonpost.com/opinions/george-will-federal-voting-drive-makes-a-mountain-out-of-a-molehill/2012/12/19/461e17c4-494c-11e2-ad54-580638ede391_story.html

18. https://www.theatlantic.com/politics/archive/2012/12/george-will-gets-almost-everything-wrong-about-voting-rights/266504/

19. Harold C. Syrett, ed., *Papers of Alexander Hamilton, Vol. 1* (New York: Columbia University Press, 1961–1979), 106.

20. Letter from John Adams to James Sullivan, May 26, 1776, https://founders.archives.gov/documents/Adams/06-04-02-0091.

21. https://thelibertarianrepublic.com/10-reasons-democracy-is-stupid/

22. Henning W. Prentis, "The Cult of Competency," *General Magazine and Historical Chronicle*, University of Pennsylvania the General Alumni Society, Vol. XLV, No. III (April 1943).

23. https://www.sourcewatch.org/index.php/National_Association_of_Manufacturers

24. http://commonsensegovernment.com/the-tytler-cycle-revisited/

25. https://townhall.com/columnists/walterewilliams/2018/11/07/skin-in-the-game-n2534984

26. https://everydayfeminism.com/2015/09/white-supremacy-everyday-life/

27. http://papers.ssrn.com/sol3/papers.cfm?abstract_id=2063742

28. http://www.ncbi.nlm.nih.gov/pmc/articles/PMC3108582/

29. http://abcnews.go.com/Health/Wellness/black-children-pain-meds-er/story?id=16231146

30. https://news.virginia.edu/content/study-racial-bias-pain-perception-appears-among-children-young-7

31. http://www.apa.org/news/press/releases/2014/03/black-boys-older.aspx

32. http://www.wsj.com/articles/SB10001424127887324432004578304463789858002

33. http://news.stanford.edu/news/2014/august/prison-black-laws-080614.html

34. http://www.eurekalert.org/pub_releases/2006-08/uog-stm081106.php

35. https://www.theguardian.com/commentisfree/2012/mar/05/new-right-ayn-rand-marx

36. https://www.nsfwcorp.com/dispatch/milton-friedman/
37. https://harpers.org/archive/2004/09/baghdad-year-zero/
38. https://www.alternet.org/2013/09/true-history-libertarianism-america-phony-ideology-promote-corporate-agenda/
39. https://reason.com/archives/1977/02/01/marketing-libertarianism
40. Ibid.
41. https://billmoyers.com/2015/07/03/social-democracy-is-100-american/
42. https://www.presidency.ucsb.edu/documents/republican-party-platform-1956
43. https://www.reaganfoundation.org/media/128614/inaguration.pdf
44. https://www.sanders.senate.gov/koch-brothers
45. http://www.loc.gov/static/programs/national-recording-preservation-board/documents/GOPACtapes.pdf
46. https://fair.org/home/language-a-key-mechanism-of-control/
47. https://www.politico.com/story/2014/04/tea-party-radio-network-105774
48. https://www.smh.com.au/politics/federal/cancer-eating-the-heart-of-australian-democracy-20180826-p4zzum.html
49. https://www.huffingtonpost.com/thom-hartmann/why-air-america-matters_b_32096.html
50. https://www.justice.gov/crt/title-42-public-health-and-welfare-chapter-20-elective-franchise-subchapter-i-h-national-voter#anchor_1973gg
51. http://clerk.house.gov/evs/1993/roll154.xml
52. https://www.senate.gov/legislative/LIS/roll_call_lists/roll_call_vote_cfm.cfm?congress=103&session=1&vote=00118#position
53. https://www.congress.gov/bill/103rd-congress/house-bill/2/text
54. https://www.supremecourt.gov/opinions/17pdf/16-980_f2q3.pdf
55. https://www.washingtonpost.com/news/post-politics/wp/2017/01/23/at-white-house-trump-tells-congressional-leaders-3-5-million-illegal-ballots-cost-him-the-popular-vote/?utm_term=.b1e68c665fb9
56. https://en.wikipedia.org/wiki/Operation_Eagle_Eye_(United_States)
57. http://archive.democrats.com/view2.cfm?id=698
58. https://www.thenation.com/article/how-the-2000-election-in-florida-led-to-a-new-wave-of-voter-disenfranchisement/
59. https://www.palmbeachpost.com/news/brett-kavanaugh-florida-ties-elian-gonzalez-and-2000-election-recount/KW4h9QMoAZd7 mogcLv7AdP/
60. https://www.theatlantic.com/politics/archive/2018/01/the-gop-just-received-another-tool-for-suppressing-votes/550052/
61. https://theintercept.com/2018/11/10/democrats-should-remember-al-gore-won-florida-in-2000-but-lost-the-presidency-with-a-preemptive-surrender/
62. http://archive3.fairvote.org/articles/raskin-a-right-to-vote/#.UNN3h4njk2I
63. https://www.govinfo.gov/content/pkg/BILLS-113hjres44ih/pdf/BILLS-113hjres44ih.pdf

64. https://www.nytimes.com/2019/06/22/upshot/america-who-deserves-representation.html

65. Wendy R. Weiser, "Voter Suppression: How Bad? (Pretty Bad)," *American Prospect*, Fall 2014, https://prospect.org/article/22-states-wave-new-voting-restrictions-threatens-shift-outcomes-tight-races.

66. https://www.ajc.com/blog/politics/ebenezer-pastor-pushes-back-sunday-voting-attack/ISDuNu8aMwOTJy09qJMCKI/

67. Weiser, "Voter Suppression: How Bad? (Pretty Bad)."

68. Brennan Center for Justice, "New Voting Restrictions in America," https://www.brennancenter.org/new-voting-restrictions-america.

69. https://www.dailykos.com/stories/2019/4/22/1852220/-Republican-states-react-to-2018-Democratic-wave-in-the-usual-way-suppressing-the-vote

70. Jonathan Brater, Kevin Morris, Myrna Pérez, Christopher Deluzio, "Purges: A Growing Threat to the Right to Vote, Brennan Center for Justice, July 20, 2018, https://www.brennancenter.org/publication/purges-growing-threat-right-vote.

71. German Lopez, "Southern States Have Closed Down at Least 868 Polling Places for the 2016 Election," Vox, November 4, 2016, https://www.vox.com/policy-and-politics/2016/11/4/13501120/vote-polling-places-elections-2016.

72. Reid Wilson, "Voter Turnout Dipped in 2016, Led by Decline among Blacks," *Hill*, May 11, 2017, https://thehill.com/homenews/campaign/332970-voter-turnout-dipped-in-2016-led-by-decline-among-blacks.

73. https://www.yahoo.com/lifestyle/opinion-stacey-abrams-being-robbed-013625104.html

74. https://staceyabrams.com/count-every-vote/

75. https://www.gregpalast.com/martin-luther-kings-cousin-blocked-from-voting/

76. Alexandra Hutzler, "Georgia Governor Race: Hillary Clinton Says If It Were a 'Fair Election,' Stacey Abrams Would Have Already Won," *Newsweek*, November 14, 2018, https://www.newsweek.com/georgia-governor-race-stacey-abrams-clinton-1215016.

77. https://www.cartercenter.org/news/features/p/elections/kenya-121517.html

78. http://www.elections.ca/content.aspx?section=res&dir=eim/issue18&document=p4&lang=e#ftn7

79. https://www.elections.ca/content.aspx?section=res&dir=eim/issue18&document=p4&lang=e#ftn6

80. https://www.theregister.co.uk/2009/08/31/german_state_election_exit_polls_leaked_on_twitter/

81. https://www.apnews.com/71a7fa094885485696aa37c3b15f993a

82. https://www.apnews.com/6eb6a4ab7b044b7798eba5675db0ac00

83. https://www.apnews.com/cf3a3c2410df444090786d215234acad
84. https://www.apnews.com/21853c2187b24ffcbb22740da4162429
85. Found by using the search terms "exit polls" and "site:bbc.com" on March 10, 2019, using Google.com—all appeared within the first seven pages of results, 10 results to the page.
86. http://content.time.com/time/politics/article/0,8599,1856081,00.html
87. https://abcnews.go.com/images/Politics/EvaluationofEdisonMitofskyElectionSystem.pdf
88. Ibid.
89. https://www.commondreams.org/views06/0601-34.htm
90. https://heavy.com/news/2016/11/2016-exit-polls-did-hillaty-clinton-win-presidential-election-voter-fraud-donald-trump-lose-rigged/
91. https://docs.google.com/spreadsheets/d/133Eb4qQmOxNvtesw2hdVns07 3R68EZx4SfCnP4IGQf8/htmlview?sle=true#gid=19 by Dave Wasserman for the Cook Political Report
92. http://www.washingtonpost.com/wp-dyn/articles/A14474-2002Jun19.html
93. https://www.sourcewatch.org/index.php/2002_Georgia_elections
94. https://www.politico.com/story/2019/02/12/georgia-voting-states-elections-1162134
95. Frank Bajak, "APNewsBreak: Georgia Election Server Wiped after Suit Filed," Associated Press, October 26, 2017, https://apnews.com/877ee1015f1c43f1965f63538b035d3f.
96. Ibid.
97. http://springfieldvt.blogspot.com/2016/11/howard-dean-hacks-central-vote.html
98. https://www.inquisitr.com/3369838/what-happened-to-howard-deans-voting-machine-interview-with-bev-harris-exposing-election-fraud/
99. https://columbusfreepress.com/article/diebold-indicted-its-spectre-still-haunts-ohio-elections
100. http://time.com/5366171/11-year-old-hacked-into-us-voting-system-10-minutes/
101. https://www.irishtimes.com/news/e-voting-machines-to-be-scrapped-1.722896
102. https://www.nytimes.com/2018/09/26/magazine/election-security-crisis-midterms.html
103. https://www.nytimes.com/2004/05/01/us/high-tech-voting-system-is-banned-in-california.html
104. https://medium.com/@jennycohn1/georgia-6-and-the-voting-machine-vendors-87278fdb0cdf
105. https://www.wired.com/2003/10/did-e-vote-firm-patch-election/
106. https://chicago.suntimes.com/news/2019/5/7/18619170/companies-raked-in-nearly-266m-from-parking-meters-other-city-assets-last-year

107. https://www.indystar.com/story/news/politics/2015/03/11/australian-company-buys-bankrupt-indiana-toll-road-vendor/70161160/
108. https://www.forbes.com/sites/katevinton/2016/06/01/these-15-billionaires-own-americas-news-media-companies/#62aa0b58660a
109. https://www.gregpalast.com/92-year-old-georgia-grandmother-purged-from-voter-rolls/
110. https://www.nytimes.com/2017/08/29/magazine/the-new-front-in-the-gerrymandering-wars-democracy-vs-math.html
111. https://www.nytimes.com/2019/06/27/us/politics/supreme-court-gerrymandering.html
112. Ibid.
113. https://www.alternet.org/news-amp-politics/how-gop-tax-cut-will-also-shrink-your-paycheck
114. https://theintercept.com/2015/07/30/jimmy-carter-u-s-oligarchy-unlimited-political-bribery/
115. http://www.theguardian.com/business/2014/nov/13/us-wealth-inequality-top-01-worth-as-much-as-the-bottom-90
116. http://www.bbc.com/news/blogs-echochambers-27074746
117. https://www.washingtonpost.com/archive/opinions/1995/01/25/why-resist-the-motor-voter-law/68dd82de-9024-4151-bdd6-55de32336ff9/?utm_term=.7de94e6bbcab
118. https://prospect.org/article/republican-war-voting
119. https://www.seattletimes.com/seattle-news/mckay-stunned-by-report-on-bush/
120. https://www.nytimes.com/2007/03/21/opinion/21iglesias.html
121. https://eagleton.rutgers.edu/wp-content/uploads/2019/07/VoterID_Turnout.pdf
122. Ibid.
123. https://www.rollingstone.com/politics/politics-news/the-gop-war-on-voting-242182/
124. https://www.propublica.org/article/kris-kobachs-lucrative-trail-of-courtroom-defeats
125. Ibid.
126. https://web.stanford.edu/group/bps/cgi-bin/wordpress/wp-content/uploads/2015/04/Do_non-citizens_vote_in_US_elections.pdf
127. https://www.cnbc.com/2018/09/11/trump-voter-suppression-attempts-are-morally-wrong-and-illegal.html
128. https://www.brennancenter.org/issues/trump-fraud-commission

Part Three: Solutions

1. https://www.pewtrusts.org/en/research-and-analysis/issue-briefs/2017/06/why-are-millions-of-citizens-not-registered-to-vote
2. https://www.nytimes.com/2019/03/05/opinion/oppression-majority.html

3. https://www.facebook.com/RepMcKinley/photos/a.130614043672264/
2136066239793691/?type=3&eid=ARDJM3UYeoPf6a6AEz9zI5rjNbn_
nvAuAWaNDWpnR58kQo8NDCUaG3JmrUDTIvMH4Eo4AAtT__
cG2oPi&__xts__%5B0%5D=
68.ARAZ1TDklWbGT6eSFBpCMIbN5zDk0zesApUDH2kZ-YNRdW-
WK2pa-xAdmcYMsEcRYjTXJrB6gkhQh4xfOPbpzlMvFOqx1Ah4aXo_
x7P6ONvuNub9fdNfs6ARa5Crws4y86p95pM5j_
TcBxZbQDG4RGvXiH4Fr2aOKjexL6JQMBuYI-
wBx1fUPiv6VFTG5-YFUVGnD5rOA3WjzaFw6EFGM3nGG53g-
8ZGDcQ8U69rdBjBRUQJcHv5mfxitL7lCXbZTiFwpmCQak3wq
3w7QGDlEr8cUMps-u4cHiqawf6pkIl7vxzw1vdnIcYWowd9Rv_
WXKXzs3EmXa7kL0kvlfe3Tv-MqQ&__tn__=EHH-R

4. https://www.foxnews.com/politics/democrats-vote-against-motion-
condemning-illegal-immigrant-voting

5. https://www.foxnews.com/politics/house-democrats-pass-sweeping-
voting-rights-bill

6. https://www.pbs.org/newshour/politics/house-passes-election-and-ethics-
overhaul-but-mcconnell-says-its-dead-on-arrival

7. https://thehill.com/policy/transportation/312055-feds-closing-driver-
license-offices-in-alabama-violates-civil-rights

8. https://www.psychologicalscience.org/news/minds-business/the-opt-out-
option.html

9. https://www.pewtrusts.org/en/research-and-analysis/issue-briefs/2017/
06/why-are-millions-of-citizens-not-registered-to-vote

10. https://www.brennancenter.org/analysis/automatic-voter-registration

11. https://www.apnews.com/07409d1e264549f093a554b38ccd82f3

12. https://www.sentencingproject.org/publications/6-million-lost-voters-
state-level-estimates-felony-disenfranchisement-2016/

13. https://www.economist.com/united-states/2018/08/09/many-states-are-
purging-voters-from-the-rolls

14. http://www.jewishpublicaffairs.org/jcpa-urges-house-members-to-
support-h-r-1-the-for-the-people-act/

15. http://www.pewresearch.org/fact-tank/2017/06/01/dislike-of-candidates-
or-campaign-issues-was-most-common-reason-for-not-voting-in-2016/

16. https://qz.com/1418567/us-elections-are-held-on-a-tuesday-thanks-to-
19th-century-farmers/

17. https://www.seniorliving.org/history/1800-1990-changes-urbanrural-us-
population/

18. https://ourworldindata.org/employment-in-agriculture

19. http://www.ncsl.org/research/elections-and-campaigns/all-mail-elections
.aspx

20. https://electionlab.mit.edu/research/voting-mail-and-absentee-voting

21. https://docs.wixstatic.com/ugdef45f5_
    13d9763efa1f4b6fb3d4a8782f98 c376.pdf
22. https://www.adn.com/alaska-news/anchorage/2018/04/04/anchorages-
    vote-by-mail-election-was-supposed-to-boost-turnout-its-now-shattered-
    a-record/
23. http://www.ncsl.org/research/elections-and-campaigns/all-mail-elections
    .aspx
24. https://www.brennancenter.org/analysis/expand-early-voting
25. Ibid.
26. https://www.organicconsumers.org/news/robert-kennedy-jr-will-next-
    election-be-hacked-electronic-voting-machines-cant-be-trusted
27. Ibid.
28. https://truthout.org/articles/privatizing-our-vote-the-ultimate-crime/
29. https://qz.com/61209/e-voting-is-failing-the-developing-world-while-
    the-us-and-europe-abandon-it/
30. https://www.washingtonpost.com/news/powerpost/paloma/
    the-cybersecurity-202/2018/09/10/the-cybersecurity-202-the-u-s-
    is-warning-congo-that-using-electronic-voting-machines-could-
    backfire/5b953d2f1b326b47ec9594d2/
31. https://www.washingtonpost.com/news/monkey-cage/wp/2016/11/17/
    the-electoral-college-badly-distorts-the-vote-and-its-going-to-get-
    worse/?utm_term=.b152d5f88cc8
32. https://www.esquire.com/news-politics/politics/a26575193/paul-lepage-
    electoral-college-white-people-say/
33. https://www.commondreams.org/views/2019/03/14/good-bye-electoral-
    college-popular-vote-movement-gaining-steam
34. https://en.wikipedia.org/wiki/Duverger%27s_law
35. https://www.huffingtonpost.com/entry/australia-compulsory-voting_
    us_5a9deac4e4b0479c02563d9a
36. https://www.futurity.org/mandatory-voting-pros-cons-1922322-2/
37. https://www.washingtonpost.com/news/politics/wp/2018/07/12/
    in-about-20-years-half-the-population-will-live-in-eight-states/?utm_
    term=.44ec59b29535
38. https://population.us/nd/
39. https://population.us/sd/
40. http://worldpopulationreview.com/states/
41. https://www.theatlantic.com/politics/archive/2013/12/dc-has-more-
    people-than-wyoming-and-vermont-still-not-a-state/437661/
42. https://en.wikipedia.org/wiki/2017_Puerto_Rican_status_referendum

ACKNOWLEDGMENTS

Special thanks go to Troy N. Miller, who worked with me for years as a producer and writer for the television show *The Big Picture*, which I hosted every weeknight for seven years in Washington, DC. Troy worked hard as a researcher, sounding board, editor, and often cowriter on parts of this book, and deserves recognition for it.

At Berrett-Koehler Publishers, Steve Piersanti—who was the founder—worked with me to kick off this series. It's been a labor of love for both of us, and I'm so grateful to Steve for his insights, rigor, and passion for this project. Of the many other people at BK who have helped with this book (and some projects associated with it), special thanks to Jeevan Sivasubramaniam (who has helped keep me sane for years) and Neal Maillet. BK is an extraordinary publishing company, and it's been an honor to have them publish my books for almost two decades.

They also provided a brilliant final editor for the book, Elissa Rabellino, who did a great job smoothing and tightening the text while also fact-checking.

Bill Gladstone, my agent for over two decades, helped make this book—and the *Hidden History* series—possible. Bill is truly one of the best in the business.

My executive producer, Shawn Taylor, helped with booking expert guests into our radio and TV programs, many of whom provided great information and anecdotes for this book. And my video producer, Nate Atwell, is a true visual genius. I'm blessed to have such a great team helping me produce a daily radio and TV program, which supports my writing work.

And, as always, my best sounding board, editor, and friend is my wife, Louise. Without her, in all probability none of my books would ever have seen the light of day.

INDEX

A

abortion, 60, 61
Abrams, Stacey, 78–81, 86, 94
absentee ballots, 31, 82, 83, 135
Adams, Abigail, 26–27
Adams, John, 9–10, 20, 27, 45, 74
Adams, John Quincey, 18
Adelson, Sheldon, 68
Affordable Care Act, 67
African American voters, suppression
    of, 5–8, 24, 39, 72, 80–82, 85–86,
    96, 99–100, 129
  "duplicate" names, 116
  ex-felons, 129
  voter ID laws and, 109
Air America, 66
Alien and Sedition Acts (1798), 20
Alito, Samuel, 70
Amendments to the Constitution
  First, 60
  Second, 24
  Thirteenth, 36, 39, 74
  Fourteenth, 24, 28, 36, 39, 75, 77
  Fifteenth, 25, 36, 39
  Nineteenth, 29, 74
  Twenty-third, 147
  Twenty-sixth, 74
American Civil Liberties Union
    (ACLU), 2, 3, 40
American exceptionalism, 148
American Legislative Exchange
    Council (ALEC), 8, 110–111
American Prospect, 82
American Revolution, 19–20
Americans for Prosperity, 65
Ames, Mark, 52
Anthony, Susan B., 28
Arnold, Benedict, 20

Ashcroft, John, 108
Asian Americans, voter suppression
    of, 110
Associated Press, 94–95
Association for Psychological Science,
    125
Atlas Shrugged (Rand), 50–51
Attucks, Crispus, 20
Australia, 65–66
  compulsory voting, 142–143
automatic voter registration, 124–127

B

"Baghdad Year Zero" (Klein), 53
Bajak, Frank, 94–95
Ballot Access and Voting Integrity
    Initiative of 2002, 108
Bancroft, Edward, 19
Bani-Sadr, Abolhassan, 6
Barkley, Alben, 25
Barkley, Gilbert, 20
Barnes, Roy, 94
Bayh, Birch, 26
Bazelon, Emily, 101
Berman, Ari, 8, 111
billionaires, 2, 4, 8–9
  libertarian oligarchs, 41, 46–47,
    50–56
  tax cuts for, 63
  trick to keep everyone from voting,
    50–56
  as white, 50. *See also* oligarchy
biometrics, 106
Bradley, Joseph P., 29
Bradwell, Myra, 29
Bradwell v. State of Illinois, 29
Bremer, L. Paul, 53–54

Brennan Center for Justice, 29–30, 101,
    125, 127, 130–131
    on early voting, 136–137
    voter suppression findings, 82–85
Brexit, 65
Breyer, Stephen, 41, 70
British Broadcasting Corporation
    (BBC), 7, 89
Brown, Donaldson, 51–52
Brown, Kate, 135
Brown, Linda, 39
Brown, Oliver, 39
Brown, Tina, 95
Brown v. Board of Education, 39–41, 60
Buckley, William F., 43
Buckley v. Valeo, 32, 60
Bump, Philip, 26
Bush, George H. W., 4
Bush, George W., 7, 23, 53, 63, 91, 95,
    107–108
    federal prosecutors, firing of,
        108–109, 117
Bush, Jeb, 7, 128
Bush v. Gore, 72–73, 74
Byrd, Harry, 40

C

caging voters, 8, 78, 130–131
California, 24, 96
    splitting to add Senators, 146
Calvin, John, 42–43
Calvinists, 41–45
campaign finance, 60, 103–106
"Cancer Eating the Heart of
    Australian Democracy" (Rudd),
    65–66
Carlson, Rachel, 2
Carrington, Edward, 34
Carter, Jimmy, 6, 19, 51, 90, 104
Carter Center, 88

Census Bureau data, 132
Center for Media and Democracy, 46
Central High School (Little Rock,
    Arkansas), 40
Chambliss, Saxby, 94, 137
Chapman, Emilee, 143
Charlottesville, Virginia, 17
Cheney, Dick, 53, 96–97, 107
Chile, 52
Chisholm, Shirley, 119
churches, black, 81–82
Churchill, Winston, 44
citizenship, proof of, 29–30, 82, 106,
    110–111, 123
Citizens United v. FEC, 32, 103, 104
Civil Rights Act of 1964, 37, 40–41
Civil War, 24, 145
Cleland, Max, 94, 137
Cleveland, Grover, 146
climate change, 105
Clinton, Bill, 58, 62, 67, 97
Clinton, Hillary, 4, 9, 85, 86, 92
Cohen, Michael, 49
college students, voter suppression of,
    81, 84, 110, 111
Common Cause, 78
commons, 1–2, 97–98
communism, rhetoric of, 50, 57
compulsory voting, 126, 142–143
Congo, 137–138
Congress, 33, 37, 54, 70–71, 79, 98
    laws stricken down by Supreme
        Court, 3
    slave states given larger share, 24
    Three-Fifths Compromise and,
        14–18, 23–24. *See also* House of
        Representatives; Senate
Constitution, 14, 21, 122
Constitutional Convention, 14, 32,
    73–74

constitutions, other countries, 75
consumer and workplace protections, 104, 105
Continental Congress, 15
Cooper v. Aaron, 40
Corker, Bob, 104
Cornuelle, Herb, 51
"corporate left," 105
crisis of legitimacy, 122
Crosscheck (Interstate Crosscheck), 115–116, 128

D

Dakota Territory, 146
Dean, Howard, 95
Declaration of Independence, 19, 27–28
democracy
  compulsory voting and, 142–143
  Friedman on, 54
  libertarian opposition to, 46–47
  Republican stance against, 121–124
Democratic Party, 6, 9, 145
  racism in roots of, 36–37
  regional split, 37
Democratic Republican Party, 36, 101
depravity, Calvinist view of, 41–42
Dessem, Larry, 113
DeVos, Betsy, 58, 97
Diebold, 95, 137
direct democracy, 10, 25
direct election, 33
disinformation campaigns, 5
District of Columbia statehood, 145–147
DMV offices, closing or limiting hours, 70, 76, 85, 123, 127
DNA analogy, 43–44
Dole, Bob, 4
double voting, 108, 114–115, 117

Dred Scott v. Sandford, 3
driver's licenses, 106
  National Voter Registration Act of 1993, 32, 69–71
Duke, David, 17
Duncan, Geoff, 94
"duplicate" voters, 115–116
Duverger's law, 142

E

Eagleton Institute of Politics at Rutgers University, 109
early voting, 136–137
Eastern States, 15
Eastland, James, 40
Economist, 132
Eisenhower, Dwight D., 40, 56–57
Election Day, 131
  national holiday proposal, 132–133
election fraud, 57, 69, 86, 88, 96
  around the world, 87–89
elections, flaws in system, 123–124
Election Studies, 113
Election Systems & Software, 95
Electoral College, 10, 15, 18–23, 41–42
  Bush v. Gore decision and, 74–75
  foreign interference, prevention of, 19–22
  national popular vote and, 140–141
  non-amendment alternatives to, 26
  slavery and, 23–26
  Three-Fifths Compromise and, 18
electoral system, 141–142
Enlightenment, 148
environmental commons, 2
environmental issues, 51
Environmental Protection Agency (EPA), 58
Equal Protection Clause, Fourteenth Amendment, 75
eugenicist beliefs, 44–45

Evenwel v. Abbott, 77–78
"e-voting," 137–138
"exact match" laws, 29, 80–81, 83, 86
exceptionalism, American, 148
ex-felons, 83, 86, 108, 127–130
exit polling, 87–93
    "adjustment" of, 91–93
    around the world, 87–89
    United States, 90–93

F

Federalist, no. 68, 21
Federalists, 19
federal prosecutors, firing of,
    108–109, 117
Federal-State Employment Service, 57
Ferguson, Grant, 127–128, 129
Ferling, John, 20
First National Bank of Boston v. Bellotti,
    60
"first past the post, winner takes all"
    electoral system, 141–142
Flake, Jeff, 104
Ford, Gerald, 4
foreign governments
    interference in U.S. politics, 19–22,
    96
    U.S. assistance to, 52
For the People Act of 2019 (H.R. 1),
    121–124, 129, 131
Foundation for Economic Education
    (FEE), 51–52, 54
founders and framers, 18, 20–23, 73–74
The Fountainhead (Rand), 51
Fox News, 65–66, 103–104, 122
France, 19, 20
Franklin, Benjamin, 10, 19
Friedman, Milton, 52, 54

G

Galton, Francis, 44
Gates, Bill, 62
Georgia, voter suppression, 78–86,
    94–96, 99–100, 137
    Georgia gubernatorial race, 78–79,
    86
Georgia Constitutional Convention,
    79
Germany, 88–89
Gerry, Elbridge, 20, 101
gerrymandering, 10, 31, 78, 100–102,
    139
Gingrich, Newt, 63, 66
Godwin, Miles E., 37
Goldstein, Daniel, 125
Goldwater, Barry, 72
GOP. *See* Republican Party
GOPAC memo, 63–64
Gore, Al, 7, 9, 74–75, 90
government
    as commons, 1
    libertarian anti-government view,
    55–60
grace, doctrine of, 43
Grant, Ulysses S., 146
Great Depression, Republican, 62, 105
Greatest Generation, 62
Great Society, 47, 58

H

hacking voting machines, 95
Haley, Nikki, 137–138
Halliburton, 96–97
Halloway, Kali, 48
Hamilton, Alexander, 20–23, 45
Hannity, Sean, 64, 65, 112
Harper's Magazine, 53
Harris, Katherine, 7
Harrison, Benjamin, 18, 146

Hayes, Rutherford B., 18
health care, 67–68
Helms, Jesse, 37
Help America Vote Act (HAVA), 93, 98–100
Hereditary Genius: An Inquiry into Its Laws and Consequences (Galton), 44
Heritage Foundation, 7, 65
Heron, Gil Scott, 145
Heyer, Heather, 17
Hispanic voters, suppression of, 5, 7–8, 72, 81, 85, 109, 114
  "duplicate" names, 116
  ex-felons, 129
Hitler, Adolf, 44
Hofeller, Thomas B., 77–78
Holocaust, 44
The Hornet's Nest (Carter), 19
House of Representatives, 141
  Democratic control of, 6
  direct election of, 33
  For the People Act of 2019 (H. R. 1), passage of, 122
  powers of, 33
  slavery's effect on, 24
Howard, Jacob, 77
Hu, Jane C., 133
Hume, Brit, 66
Husted, John, 70
Husted v. Randolph, 70
Hyde Amendment, 60

I

Iglesias, David, 109
"illegal aliens," 5, 71–72, 106–107
  as business venture, 111–113
Indian Citizenship Act (1924), 30
individual action, need for, 148–149
intelligence services, 96

Internet voting, 137–138
Iowa, prosecution of ex-felons, 127–128
Iran-Contra, 6
Iran hostages, 6
Iraq, 53–54
Ireland, 95–96, 137

J

Jackson, Andrew, 25
Jefferson, Thomas, 19–20, 27, 34
Jim Crow, modern day, 86
Jobs, Steve, 62
John Birch Society (JBS), 50, 51–52, 57
Johnson, Eric J., 125
Johnson, Lyndon, 6, 37–38, 40
Jordan, Christine, 86, 99–100
Jordan, Michael, 50
Justice Department, 80, 108

K

Kavanaugh, Bret, 73
Kaye, Harvey J., 56
Kemp, Brian, 80–81, 83–86, 94, 100
Kennedy, John F., 61
Kennedy, Robert F., Jr., 137
Kenya, 88–89
Kercheval, Samuel, 34
Kerry, John, 90–91
King, Martin Luther, Jr., 86, 99
King, Rufus, 15
Klein, Naomi, 53
Kobach, Kris, 111–114, 128
Koch, David, 51, 58–60
Koch, Fred, 50, 51
Koch network, 4, 8, 46, 68, 104
Koch oil operation, 51
Korbmacher, Mrs. (victim of religious superstition), 14, 16–17

"Kris Kobach's Lucrative Trail of Courtroom Defeats" (ProPublica), 112–113
Kroy, Moshe, 54–55, 59
Ku Klux Klan, 17, 80

L
"Language: A Key Mechanism of Control" (GOPAC), 63–64
League of Women Voters, 2, 83
A Leap in the Dark: The Struggle to Create the American Republic (Ferling), 20
LePage, Paul, 41–42, 141
Levin, Mark, 64, 65
libertarian oligarchs, 41, 46–47, 50–56
    anti-government view, 55–60
Libertarian Party, 51
    platform, 1980, 59–60
Limbaugh, Rush, 64, 65
Lincoln, Abraham, 36, 145, 146
literacy, 135
lobbying, 51–52, 54, 110
    privatization and, 97–98
local elections, 122
Lofgren, Zoe, 122

M
Madison, James, 15–16, 32–33
mail, voting by, 133–136
Manafort, Paul, 4
The Manchurian Candidate (film), 19
Marbury decision (1803), 3
Marshall, Thurgood, 40
"Massive Resistance" movement, 39–40
McCain, John, 67
McConnell, Mitch, 122, 129
McKay, John, 108–109
McKinley, David, 121–122

media, 64–67, 104, 105
Medicare, 47, 58, 67
Mercer, Robert, 68
Meredith v. Jefferson County Board of Education, 41
mergers, corporate, 105
middle class, 62
midterm elections, 2018, 68, 130
military functions, privatization of, 96–97
Millar, Fran, 82
Mississippi Burning (film), 38
MIT Election Data + Science Lab, 134
Mitofsky, Warren, 90, 92–93
"model legislation," 8, 110–111
Monbiot, George, 50–51
money, role in politics, 103–106, 124
Monroe Elementary School (Topeka, Kansas), 39
Motor Voter Act (1993), 32, 69–71, 106–107
Moyers, Bill, 38, 56
Moyers on America (Moyers), 38
MSNBC, 30
Murdoch, Rupert, 65–66, 103–104

N
Nader, Ralph, 2
names, "duplicate," 115–116
Nation, 8
National Association for the Advancement of Colored People (NAACP), 39
National Association of Manufacturers, 46
National Association of Real Estate Boards, 54
National Conference of State Legislatures (NCSL), 134
National Guard, 40

National Organization for Women
    (NOW), 29
national popular vote, 140–141
National Rifle Association, 62
National Voter Registration Act of
    1993, 32, 69–71, 106–107
Native Americans, vote and, 26–28,
    30–32, 135
    tribal IDs, 31
Nelson, Herbert, 54
Nevada statehood, 145–146
New York, 24
    splitting to add senators, 146
New York Times, 8, 77, 96, 123
Ney, Bob, 98–99
Nixon, Richard, 2, 6, 38, 72
    "law and order" and "silent
        majority" campaigns, 49
    "Southern strategy," 38, 57
    treason, 103
non-landowners, 10
*Notes of Debates in the Federal
    Convention of 1787* (Madison),
    15–16, 32

O

Obama, Barack, 17, 67, 81, 85
Obergefell v. Hodges, 68–69
Ocasio-Cortez, Alexandria, 148
O'Dell, Wally, 95
Ohio, voter suppression, 7–8, 70–71,
    73, 95
oligarchy, 4–5, 32–34
    libertarian, 41, 46–47
    money, role in politics, 103–106
    property rights and, 32–33. *See also*
        billionaires; Republican Party
Operation Eagle Eye, 72–73, 76
opt-out *vs.* opt-in choices, 125–126
Orange Revolution, 88
organ donors, 125

P

Paine, Thomas, 2, 10
Palast, Greg, 9, 99–100
paper ballots, 88–89, 137–139
*Parents Involved in Community Schools
    v. Seattle School District No. 1*, 41
partisan gridlock, 141–142
passports, 106
Pelosi, Nancy, 121
Pena, Lito, 72
Pence, Mike, 5
Pennsylvania Packet, 14
Perdue, Sonny, 94
Perry, Rich, 111
persons, rights of, 32
Pew surveys, 122, 125, 132
Philadelphia, Mississippi, 38, 126
Philadelphia, Pennsylvania, 14
Pinckneym Charles, 16
Pine Ridge Reservation, South
    Dakota, 31
Plessy v. Ferguson, 3, 39
Pocan, Mark, 75, 110
Polis, Jared, 140
Politico, 64, 94
polls, closing of, 5, 81–82, 85
poor, as defective, 45
Powell, Lewis, 2–4, 60, 103
Prentis, Henning W., Jr., 46
Presidential Advisory Commission on
    Election Integrity, 117
presidential elections
    1792, 132
    1800, 20
    1812, 101
    1872, 28
    1956, 56–57
    1968, 6, 38
    1980, 6–7, 90
    2000, 6–7, 46, 72, 75, 90, 92–93, 99

presidential elections *(continued)*
  2004, 90–91, 92–93, 108–109
  2008, 17
  2016, 4–8, 38, 68, 71–72, 84–85, 92
primary system, 142
prisons, privatization of, 97
"private academies," 40
privatization, 52–54
  of voting machines, 96–98
The Proper Sphere of Government
  (Spencer), 43–44
property rights, 32–33
ProPublica, 112–113
provisional ballots, 86, 98–100
  ex-felons and, 128
Pruitt, Scott, 58
Puerto Rico statehood, 147

R

racism, 4–5
  of Democratic Party, 36–37
  legacy of Civil Rights Act, 38
  myths and stereotypes, 16–17
  Three-Fifths Compromise, 14–16
  Trump and, 68
  why racists don't want everyone to
    vote, 36–38.
    See also white supremacists
Radical Republicans, 36
Rand, Ayn, 47, 50–51
Randolph, Edmund, 15, 17
ranked-choice, or instant-runoff
  voting system, 141–142
Raskin, Jamie, 75
Read, Leonard, 52
Reagan, Ronald, 4, 7, 38, 46, 58, 63, 72,
  90, 112
  treason committed by, 6
Reagan administration, 34
Reaganomics/Reaganism, 6, 62
Reason magazine, 54–55

redistricting, 77–78
  nonpartisan commissions, 102.
    See also gerrymandering
red shift, 90–93
Refugee Relief Act, 57
refugees, 57
Rehnquist, William, 7, 72
religion, as racism, 5
representatives, 2
Republican National Convention,
  204, 111–112
Republican Party, 2, 4–9
  consent decree, 1981, 73
  For the People Act, opposition to,
    121–124
  Radical Republicans, 36
  secretaries of state, 5, 7, 9, 92
  Senate, control of, 69, 122, 124, 129
  stand against voting and
    democracy, 120–121
  Supreme Court, control of, 7–9
  voter suppression by, 2, 7–10
resegregation, 39, 41
Revolutionary War, 27
Riggs, Sarah, 94
right-left battle, 2
right to vote not codified, 73–76, 117,
  122, 131
Roberts, John, 41, 73
Roe v. Wade, 4, 60
Roosevelt, Franklin Delano, 56
Rosenbaum, Alisa Zinovyevna
  (Ayn Rand). *See also* Rand, Ayn
Rossi, Dino, 108–109
Rove, Karl, 107–108
Rudd, Kevin, 65
Rumsfeld, Donald, 53
Russell, Richard, 37
Russia, 52
Ryan, Paul, 75–76

S

Sanders, Bernie, 58, 67, 130
Schwerner, Goodman, and Chaney,
    126
Second Bill of Rights, 56
secretaries of state, Republican, 5, 7,
    9, 92
Senate
    Democratic control of, 6, 145
    Electoral College proposals and,
        25–26
    inadequate representation of
        people, 25–26, 146–147
    Republican, 69, 122, 124, 129
    Three-Fifths Compromise and,
        24–25
"separate but equal," 39
Shelby County v. Holder, 73, 85, 130
Sherman, Roger, 18
"skin in the game" argument, 47
slave patrols, 17
slavery, Electoral College and, 23–26
small-population states, 24, 26
social Darwinism, reverse, 44
socialism, rhetoric of, 50
social issues, 60–63
Social Security, 58, 127
Social Security numbers, 128
social welfare programs, billionaire
    opposition to, 47, 50
solutions, 11
    activism, 148–149
    automatic voter registration,
        124–127
    compulsory voting, 142–143
    early voting, extension of, 136–137
    Election Day as national holiday,
        132–133
    Electoral College and national
        popular vote, 140–141
    end voter caging, 130–131
    ex-felons, restoring rights of,
        127–130
    mail, voting by, 133–136
    non-amendment alternative to
        Electoral College, 26
    paper ballots or receipts, 137–139
    For the People Act of 2019 (H.R. 1),
        121–124, 129, 131
    stop politicians from choosing
        voters, 139
    two-party system, getting beyond,
        141–142
Sotomayor, Sonia, 71
"Southern Manifesto" (1956), 40
Southern states
    Brown v. Board of Education and, 40
    Three-Fifths Compromise and,
        14–18, 23–24
"Southern strategy" (Nixon), 38, 57
Soviet Union, 52
Spain, 19
Spencer, Herbert, 43–44
spoof sites, 137
sterilization laws, 44
Stevens, John Paul, 41
stock exchange crash of 1929, 103
Sullivan, James, 9
Supreme Court, 2–4
    amicus curiae briefs, 3
    gerrymandering rulings, 101–102,
        139
    Republican, 7–9
    voter suppression and, 7–8
    voter suppression of Native
        Americans, 31.
        *See also individual Supreme Court
        decisions*
Sweden, 126
swing states, 141

T

talk radio, 64–65

tax cuts for wealthy, 63, 68

Telecommunications Act (1996), 97

Thatcher, Samuel, 25

Three-Fifths Compromise, 14–18, 23–24

Thurmond, Strom, 37

Tillman Act (1907), 103

Topic A show (CNBC), 95

Townhall, 47

treason, 6, 57, 76

Truman, Harry, 25, 67

Trump, Donald, 4, 18, 63, 67–68
   Electoral College and, 23, 119
   exit polls and, 92
   "illegal alien" rhetoric, 71–72
   on Obama's election, 17
   racism of, 49
   voter fraud myth and, 113, 117

Trump, Donald, Jr., 38

two-party system, 141–142

Tyler, John, 132

Tytler, Alexander, 46

"Tytler Cycle," 46

U

Ukraine, 87, 88

unconditional election, Calvinist, 41–42

unregistered voters, 125

US Census Bureau, 30

US Chamber of Commerce memo (Powell), 2–4, 103

V

Vermont, 24

Vespa, Matt, 140

Vietnam, 6

Virginia
   Massive Resistance, 40
   slaveholders as presidents, 23

Vogel, Ken, 64–65

vote, as commons, 1–2

voter apathy, as result of loss of representation, 106

voter ID laws, 5–6, 8, 82–84, 109–110
   women, effect on, 29–30

voter intimidation, 7, 72–73

voter purging, 5, 7–9, 70–71, 84, 85, 123
   "duplicate" names, 115–116
   for names similar to ex-felons, 128, 129

voter registration, 8, 83, 123
   automatic, 124–127
   go-to-prison threats, 84
   opt-out choice, 125–126

voter suppression, 2, 4–7, 69
   2015–2016 laws, 82–84
   District of Columbia and Puerto Rico, 145–147
   "Massive Resistance" movement and, 39–40
   "model legislation," 8, 110–111
   Native Americans and, 30–32
   numbers, not voters, 76–78
   Operation Eagle Eye, 72–73, 76
   poor as defective, 45
   in Southern states, 24
   women affected by, 29–30.
   See also caging voters; "exact match" laws; ex-felons; exit polling; gerrymandering; polls, closing of; provisional ballots; voter purging; voting machines

voting
   new war on, 69–73
   right to vote not codified, 73–76, 117, 122

voting, importance of, 1–2

voting fraud, myth of, 2, 71–72, 106–111
    as dogma, 107–111
    as mission, 111–114
voting machines, 93–96, 124
    privatization, 96–98
Voting Rights Act of 1965, 5, 31, 37, 78
    Georgia and, 80
    gutting of, 2013, 5–6, 41, 73, 130

W

wages, 9
Walker, Scott, 8
Wallace, George, 36–37
Wanniski, Jude, 4
"The War on Voting Is a War on
    Women" (MSNBC), 30
Washington Post, 26, 38, 44, 88,
    106–107, 137–138, 140
Watergate investigations, 103
Weinger, Mackenzie, 64–65
Weiser, Wendy, 82
Welch, Robert, 51
Weyrich, Paul, 4, 7, 116
Whig Party, 36
white supremacist groups, police
    investigation numbers, 17

white supremacists, 17, 48–49
    Brown v. Board of Education and,
        39–40
    fear of nonwhite vote, 41–42.
        See also racism
"Why I Was Fired" (Iglesias), 109
Will, George, 43, 44–45
Williams, Walter E., 47
Wilson, James, 17
Wilson, Pete, 107
Wilson, Woodrow, 44
Winfrey, Oprah, 50
women
    no legal existence for, 28–29
    vote and, 26–28, 54, 74
    voter suppression, effects on, 29–30
Wu, Tim, 123
Wyoming, 24

X

XYZ Affair, 20

Y

Yanukovych, Viktor, 88
Yushchenko, Viktor, 87, 88

ABOUT THE AUTHOR

© Ian Sbalcio

Thom Hartmann is the four-time Project Censored Award–winning, *New York Times* best-selling author of more than 25 books currently in print in over a dozen languages on five continents in the fields of psychiatry, ecology, politics, and economics, and the number one progressive-talk-show host in the United States.

His daily three-hour radio/TV show is syndicated on commercial radio stations nationwide, on nonprofit and community stations nationwide and in Europe and Africa by Pacifica, across the entire North American continent on SiriusXM Satellite Radio, on its own YouTube channel, via podcast, on Facebook Live, worldwide through the US American Forces Network, and through the Thom Hartmann app in the App Store and for Android. The show is also simulcast as TV in real time into over 60 million US homes by the Free Speech TV network on Dish Network, DirecTV, and cable TV systems nationwide.

He has helped set up hospitals, famine relief programs, schools, and refugee centers in India, Uganda, Australia, Colombia, Russia, Israel, and the United States. Formerly rostered with the state of Vermont as a psychotherapist, founder of the Michigan Healing Arts Center, and licensed as an NLP Trainer by Richard Bandler, he was the originator of the revolutionary Hunter/Farmer Hypothesis to understand attention deficit hyperactivity disorder (ADHD).

In the field of environmentalism, Thom has cowritten and costarred in four documentaries with Leonardo DiCaprio, and is also featured in his documentary theatrical releases *The 11th Hour* and *Ice on Fire*. His book *The Last Hours of Ancient Sunlight*, about the end of the age of oil and the inspiration for *The 11th Hour*, is an international best seller and used as a textbook in many schools.

Thom lives with his wife of 48 years, Louise, and their two dogs and three cats, on the Columbia River in Portland, Oregon. They're the parents of three adult children.

BOOKS BY THOM HARTMANN

The Hidden History of Guns and the Second Amendment

The Hidden History of the Supreme Court and the Betrayal of America

ADD: A Different Perception

Adult ADHD: How to Succeed as a Hunter in a Farmer's World

The Last Hours of Ancient Sunlight:The Fate of the World and What We Can Do Before It's Too Late

Unequal Protection: How Corporations Became "People"—and How You Can Fight Back

The Crash of 2016: The Plot to Destroy America—and What We Can Do to Stop It

Screwed: The Undeclared War Against the Middle Class—and What We Can Do About It

Rebooting the American Dream: 11 Ways to Rebuild Our Country

The Thom Hartmann Reader

Walking Your Blues Away: How to Heal the Mind and Create Emotional Well-Being

The Prophet's Way: A Guide to Living in the Now

Legacy of Secrecy: The Long Shadow of the JFK Assassination (with Lamar Waldron)

Cracking the Code: How to Win Hearts, Change Minds, and Restore America's Original Vision

We the People: A Call to Take Back America

What Would Jefferson Do?: A Return to Democracy

Threshold: The Progressive Plan to Pull America Back from the Brink

The Last Hours of Humanity: Warming the World to Extinction

The American Revolution of 1800: How Jefferson Rescued Democracy from Tyranny and Faction (with Dan Sisson)

ADD Success Stories: A Guide to Fulfillment for Families with Attention Deficit Disorder

Ultimate Sacrifice: John and Robert Kennedy, the Plan for a Coup in Cuba, and the Murder of JFK (with Lamar Waldron)

Attention Deficit Disorder: A Different Perception

Think Fast: The ADD Experience

Healing ADD: Simple Exercises That Will Change Your Daily Life

Thom Hartmann's Complete Guide to ADHD: Help for Your Family at Home, School and Work

From the Ashes: A Spiritual Response to the Attack on America (anthology)

Air America: The Playbook (anthology)

Beyond ADD: Hunting for Reasons in the Past and Present

The Best of the Desktop Publishing Forum on Compuserve (anthology)

The Greatest Spiritual Secret of the Century

Death in the Pines: An Oakley Tyler Novel

Also in the Hidden History Series

The Hidden History of Guns and the Second Amendment

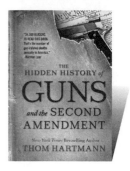

Thom Hartmann, the most popular progressive radio host in America and a *New York Times* bestselling author, reveals the real history of guns in America and what we can do to limit both their lethal impact and the power of the gun lobby. Taking an in-depth, historically informed view, Hartmann examines the brutal role guns have played in American history, from the genocide of the Native Americans to the enforcement of slavery and post–Civil War racism, coining the term "the Unholy Trinity of racism, genocide, and guns." He also exposes the alliance of the NRA and conservative Supreme Court justices that invented the unlimited right to own guns. Ever practical, Hartmann identifies solutions that can break the power of the gun lobby and put an end to the alarming reality of gun violence in the United States.

Paperback, 192 pages, ISBN 978-1-5230-8599-6
Digital PDF, ISBN 978-1-5230-8600-9
Digital ePub, ISBN 978-1-5230-8601-6
Digital audio, ISBN 978-1-5230-8603-0

Berrett–Koehler Publishers, Inc.
www.bkconnection.com   **800.929.2929**

Also in the Hidden History Series

The Hidden History of the Supreme Court and the Betrayal of America

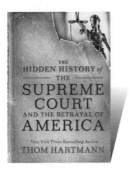

This volume of Thom Hartmann's explosive series of hidden histories critiques the omnipotent Supreme Court and offers pathways toward returning power to the people. Taking his typically in-depth, historically informed view, Hartmann asks, What if the Supreme Court didn't have the power to strike down laws? According to the Constitution, it doesn't. From the founding of the republic until 1803, the Supreme Court was the final court of appeals, as it was always meant to be. Hartmann argues it is not the role of the Supreme Court to decide what the law is but rather the people themselves who vote at the ballot box. America does not belong to the kings and queens of the Court; it belongs to us.

Paperback, 192 pages, ISBN 978-1-5230-8594-1
PDF ebook, ISBN 978-1-5230-8596-5
ePub ebook, ISBN 978-1-5230-8597-2
Digital audio, ISBN 978-1-5230-8595-8

Berrett–Koehler Publishers, Inc.
www.bkconnection.com   **800.929.2929**

Berrett–Koehler
Publishers

Berrett-Koehler is an independent publisher dedicated to an ambitious mission: *Connecting people and ideas to create a world that works for all.*

Our publications span many formats, including print, digital, audio, and video. We also offer online resources, training, and gatherings. And we will continue expanding our products and services to advance our mission.

We believe that the solutions to the world's problems will come from all of us, working at all levels: in our society, in our organizations, and in our own lives. Our publications and resources offer pathways to creating a more just, equitable, and sustainable society. They help people make their organizations more humane, democratic, diverse, and effective (and we don't think there's any contradiction there). And they guide people in creating positive change in their own lives and aligning their personal practices with their aspirations for a better world.

And we strive to practice what we preach through what we call "The BK Way." At the core of this approach is *stewardship,* a deep sense of responsibility to administer the company for the benefit of all of our stakeholder groups, including authors, customers, employees, investors, service providers, sales partners, and the communities and environment around us. Everything we do is built around steward-ship and our other core values of *quality, partnership, inclusion,* and *sustainability.*

This is why Berrett-Koehler is the first book publishing company to be both a B Corporation (a rigorous certification) and a benefit corpora-tion (a for-profit legal status), which together require us to adhere to the highest standards for corporate, social, and environmental perfor-mance. And it is why we have instituted many pioneering practices (which you can learn about at www.bkconnection.com), including the Berrett-Koehler Constitution, the Bill of Rights and Responsibilities for BK Authors, and our unique Author Days.

We are grateful to our readers, authors, and other friends who are supporting our mission. We ask you to share with us examples of how BK publications and resources are making a difference in your lives, organizations, and communities at www.bkconnection.com/impact.

Dear reader,

Thank you for picking up this book and welcome to the worldwide BK community! You're joining a special group of people who have come together to create positive change in their lives, organizations, and communities.

What's BK all about?

Our mission is to connect people and ideas to create a world that works for all.

Why? Our communities, organizations, and lives get bogged down by old paradigms of self-interest, exclusion, hierarchy, and privilege. But we believe that can change. That's why we seek the leading experts on these challenges—and share their actionable ideas with you.

A welcome gift

To help you get started, we'd like to offer you a free copy of one of our bestselling ebooks:

www.bkconnection.com/welcome

When you claim your **free ebook,** you'll also be subscribed to our blog.

Our freshest insights

Access the best new tools and ideas for leaders at all levels on our blog at ideas.bkconnection.com.

Sincerely,

Your friends at Berrett-Koehler